FIVE
LONDON
PIANO MAKERS

Front cover illustration:

'The British piano of the BBC'
The Challen model 19 grand (6' 4" long)

[Author's collection]

Rear cover:

Stringing a Challen baby grand at Hermitage Road,
circa 1960

[Author's collection]

FIVE LONDON PIANO MAKERS

BRINSMEAD
CHALLEN • COLLARD
DANEMANN • WELMAR

ALASTAIR LAURENCE

Published by the author

in association with

Keyword Press
291 Sprowston Mews
London E7 9AE
England

http://www.keywordpress.co.uk

First published 2010

ISBN 978-0-9555590-1-3

British Library Cataloguing in Publication Data

A catalogue record for this book is available from the British Library

Printed by
Pioneer Press Limited
Skipton
North Yorkshire
BD23 2TZ

CONTENTS

ACKNOWLEDGEMENTS

THE author wishes to express his gratitude for the valuable information, or advice, or illustrative material, received from the following individuals:

Patrick and Ann Billinghurst; Patrick Booth; Chris and Coral Brinsmead; George Brinsmead; Rev. Keith Brinsmead; Bryan Brown; Richard and Katrina Burnett; Katherine Challen; Peter Challen; Richard Chapman; Sue Christian; John Collard; Edgar Danemann; Peter Danemann; Oliver Davies; Jeff Gardner; Charles Gilbey; David Holmes; Brian Kemble; Bill Kibby; David Locke; Donald Lyon; George McCrone; Jenny Nex; Sydney Paradine; Les Pearce; William Sale; Horace Singleton; Edmund Whomes; Roger Willson; Jacqui Winchester; and Margaret Wolfe-Barry.

Last but not least, the author wishes to extend his thanks to Peter Bavington of *Keyword Press,* who has been of great help and support with the long chore of compiling this book. He has scrutinised the draft manuscript, and made many helpful observations and suggestions along the way.

INTRODUCTION

THIS book records the histories of five well-known piano manufacturers, and is the end product of over forty years' research by the author into London piano making.

The origin of each firm is examined, and then the way in which each company developed its own distinctive musical product is looked at in some detail. The various piano-making personalities, whose musical, technical and business skills lay behind the success of their respective enterprises, are introduced from time to time as the account proceeds. Reference is made, not only to some of the stylistic features of particular instruments, but also to the curious and often unique technical processes carried out in order to manufacture them. Details of the interesting factory buildings, and the hard-working London craftsmen who occupied them, form an important part of the narrative.

Although many different archive sources have been consulted in order to try and build up an accurate account, most of the information contained in the following pages has been gleaned from anecdotes told to the author by word of mouth from elderly members of the industry, most of whom have long passed on. This book could therefore be described as a 'record', preserving something of the unwritten folk history surrounding London piano manufacture, and the fascinating and often important information that such folk history holds. The author, well aware that he is likely to be the only person surviving who remembers most of the stories, is pleased to commit them to print, and so prevent them from becoming lost forever.

The question may well be asked: why have these five particular firms been chosen for this book? What about other equally-important London piano makers, such as Broadwood or Chappell? It just so happens that the author's lines of research have so far been most fruitful concerning the five makers which are the subject of this book. At least enough information has been assembled to justify a detailed chapter about each one; and the five firms represent a good cross-section of the industry, ranging from an 'ancient' company like Collard and Collard, with its roots back in the eighteenth century, to others like Danemann and Welmar, which were essentially twentieth-century enterprises.

There were two things that all five firms had in common: they all made good-quality instruments; and they all made concert grands, which in their day were among the finest keyboard instruments obtainable by the music profession. In this respect, the five makers have each in their own way played an important role in the musical culture of the nation. All five were family-run businesses – usually with at least three generations of the same family involved, and often involved in a very practical way with piano design and construction. This latter fact alone helps to make their histories more interesting.

Writing this book has been, it is true, a lonely and depressing exercise, mainly because of the fact that all five piano makers have now vanished without trace, and any instruments still made bearing their trademarks are now sourced in the Far East. The near-total collapse of British piano making means that there seems to be little likelihood of those fascinating centres of musical workmanship – the small piano factories – ever being seen again on these shores. All of which must make life a little more meaningless, and limit the opportunities, for those of a younger generation with musical craft skills seeking interesting employment.

More worrying and depressing is the fact that the transmission of specialised piano-making knowledge, the kind of knowledge which cannot be learnt from a book, has come to an end in Britain. The erosion of skill, on a national level, as a result of the decline in manufacturing of all kinds, is a matter which currently appears to be of little concern to politicians and captains of industry alike, blinded as they are by the 'headless' and unprincipled energy of global market forces.

The author very much hopes that within a few years he will be able to find the time and energy to present the reader with a companion to this book – a 'volume 2' – dealing with other London piano makers, including, of course, Broadwood and Chappell. He also hopes that in the same future publication, he might be able to report some good news: the news of the emergence of a new, small but thriving, piano-making industry, perhaps at craft workshop level, arising out of the ashes of an honourable and once-great London tradition.

Finchcocks
Goudhurst
Kent

January 2010

John Brinsmead (1814-1908).

[A portrait painted by his grandson, A. J. Billinghurst]

1
JOHN BRINSMEAD & SONS

THE history of the Brinsmead company revolves around a very remarkable personality, John Brinsmead (1814-1908), a Devonian who was born in the village of Weare Giffard, near Bideford. Brinsmead had phenomenal stamina. His exceptional skills in joinery and cabinet making were combined with an uncanny ability to work at high speed. He had huge ambition and a huge ego to go with it. He had a dominating personality, and later in life controlled his toiling factory workforce with a rod of iron; but he was nevertheless kindly and charming, and was concerned for the welfare of his employees. He was clever in the use of money; and last but not least, he had a remarkable flair for self-publicity. In short, he had all the qualities necessary to become a very successful piano manufacturer in Victorian London.

It comes as something of a surprise, therefore, when we learn that Brinsmead's early career had absolutely nothing whatsoever to do with pianos. As a teenager living in the rustic backwater of Weare Giffard, Brinsmead's only ambition was to become a farmer. He carefully saved up his pocket money, and by the time he was in his late teens was able to buy his own flock of sheep. He would accompany his flock on to the local common, where he would while away the time playing folk melodies to the long-suffering animals on his rustic pipe. In fact, all members of the Brinsmead family appeared to be musicians of one kind or another, and this helps to explain John's later fascination with keyboard ivories rather than with woolly fleeces.

It was John's elder brother Henry who triggered Brinsmead's interest in piano construction. Henry had moved to London by the early 1830s, and in the year 1835 he opened his own small workshop building new pianos. He was soon joined by his younger brother 'up from the country', who by then had clearly lost interest in his sheep and was immersed in the glamours of new pianos. Henry's skills were focussed on the internal mechanism and stringing of the piano, whilst John's skills were primarily involved in woodwork, soundboard making, and the construction of the outer casework. After a couple of years of working together, the two brothers apparently fell out, and John left to establish his own piano-making business in a very small way (1837) with only a couple of assistants. Henry continued in business, maintaining his own workshop until around the year 1880.

John's early instruments were straight-strung uprights with the customary over-damper sticker actions of the period. Grand pianomaking came much later on in his firm's history, as did that curiosity, the 'Top Tuner' upright (which was largely the invention of Brinsmead's eldest son, Thomas).

John Brinsmead's extraordinary stamina may be demonstrated by his typical working day in the closing decades of the nineteenth century: he got out of bed at his house near Regent's Park at around 6am each morning, threw on his old working clothes, and set off walking the two-mile trek to his factory in Grafton Road, Kentish Town. On reaching the factory at about seven o'clock, he would make a tour of inspection, check the work in progress in all departments, and finally look over the finished instruments awaiting despatch. Once he was satisfied that all was in order, he would walk the two-mile journey back to his home and sit down to a hearty breakfast at some time between eight and nine. Following breakfast, he would change into the smartest of gentlemanly attire, and then set off walking in a southerly direction through Regent's Park until he reached the firm's showrooms at 18-22 Wigmore Street, where he would spend the rest of the working day supervising sales and meeting clients.

His enforced daily walks certainly helped to keep Brinsmead's health in good shape. In fact, his health and stamina was in such good shape that Brinsmead did not stop walking – not until he had reached the remarkably-advanced age of ninety in October 1904, when he felt it was time to take life a little more easily and retire. Nevertheless, for a further three years until his death at the age of ninety-three, he was always present at the weekly board meeting of the company each Thursday. His regular walks were almost certainly welcomed; they probably enabled him to 'clear his head' and take a respite from running a complicated, taxing and extensive business, with all its stresses.

The workroom in the Grafton Road factory in which John made the final inspection of his firm's instruments was called by his workforce *The Chamber of Horrors*. This name was obviously derived from London's well-known tourist attraction, Madam Tussaud's waxworks, in which a basement room, the Chamber of Horrors, houses the gruesome wax effigies of sordid criminal life. The misfortune for any worker being summoned to Brinsmead's own Chamber of Horrors in the piano factory meant that he would expect to receive the horror of a severe reprimand from Mr Brinsmead himself for any construction work carried out in an unsatisfactory way. Dismissal would no doubt be threatened if the employee in question did not 'pull his socks up'.

Brinsmead was clearly aiming for high standards. He could be a hard taskmaster in true Victorian fashion, and so his workers might be described as 'loyal but long-suffering'. It was in this same 'Chamber of Horrors' that John Brinsmead himself carried out the final voicing of the felt hammer heads of each piano (with needles). Alfred Squire, writing in 1904, stated: 'It is a well-known fact that as a toner or voicer of a piano he stands without a rival. He is a master in the knowledge of what tone should be and how to obtain it from the hammer. Every piano [produced in the factory] he tried and toned, and if he erred at all it was on the refined side of tone quality'.[1]

We can guess that John Brinsmead's bullying and browbeating extended to the three of his four sons who one-by-one dutifully entered the business. They no doubt suffered in similar fashion to the toiling workforce when things were not quite right. Thomas, the eldest son (known to everyone in the Trade as 'Tom'), in charge of production at Grafton Road, became seriously ill in the late 1890s – probably with a stress-related illness – and his doctor advised him to take a long rest from factory chores. The youngest son, Horace, was pushed by his father to travel the world in order to promote the firm's products. Horace could be found in Philadelphia, USA, in 1876; Sydney, Australia (1879) and Melbourne, Australia (1880-1881). The third son, Edgar, had the misfortune of the handicap of slowly-increasing blindness, but this did not prevent him from taking an active role in the firm, nor from writing the well-known treatise *History of the Pianoforte,* which we shall discuss shortly.

John Brinsmead's flair for self-publicity became famous and was in all probability disliked by most members of the British piano trade. Old-established and more conservative firms such as Broadwood and Collard

Brinsmead family group, circa 1885.
Left to right: Thomas James (seated), Sydney, Mrs Susan Brinsmead (seated),
Laura, Horace George, Emily, Mr John Brinsmead (seated),
Edgar William, Rosa (Mrs Billinghurst).
[Photo: Chris and Coral Brinsmead's archive]

must have sneered at the vulgarity, lack of taste, and self-praise found in Brinsmead's advertising promotions; but such advertisements were only emulating the kind of self-publicity already commonly found among American and German piano makers, where Bechstein in particular was constantly 'puffing' and name-dropping. There was hardly a crowned head in Europe who did not have the pleasure of the ownership of a Bechstein grand; and Carl Bechstein himself, with his huge ego, was determined to make sure that the world knew of this fact.[2] There is no doubt, however, that the large amount of successful publicity carried out by the Brinsmead company during the last three decades of the nineteenth century significantly contributed to the company's ever-increasing sales.

The Brinsmead firm's numerous patents, which were taken out for improvements in piano action design, were usually described as being for *perfect check repeater action*. We sometimes wonder how many patents were actually necessary as one new type of repeater action apparently became even more perfect than the last. In fact, on one occasion, Brinsmead's newly-invented mechanism was *too perfect* – it imparted too powerful a hammer blow to the strings, and so the strings themselves had to be strengthened by use of thicker wire.[3]

A rival maker was the Paris firm of Erard (which had a branch and factory in London). On one occasion, the date of which was not recorded for posterity, Erards decided to run a special promotion featuring sixteen of its large concert grands at a public concert at the Royal Aquarium. Not to be outdone, John Brinsmead hired the Royal Albert Hall, and announced his own monumental event which would feature *fifty* Brinsmead grand pianos, each instrument having two players, making a total of one hundred simultaneously-performing pianists.

The journalist Alfred Squire, writing in the *British and Colonial Piano Journal* of December 1904, gives us a few more details of this extraordinary event:

> *All the pianos were tuned to standard pitch. When the 'piano band' started, we could not understand where such solid volumes of tone came from; every corner of this great Hall was full of music; the sound waves seemed so to penetrate and fill the place that everything seemed to vibrate – the power of the euphonious tone seemed forced upon you. We can only give the reasons in this way: there are two hundred hands; and if every hand puts down four notes at one time, this makes 800 notes struck at the same time, and all being well in tune the symphony becomes greater; and when they put down the fifty pedals it seemed to really lift the roof. Another peculiar feature: although the power of tone was great, it did not in any way seem to grate upon the hearing or in any way produce a singing in the ears; the tone was marvellously pure and held the sound waves, like the double bass over the full brass band. The fifty pianos told out well in Wagner's celebrated* Tannhauser *march.*

The comments of the tuners who were obliged to toil for hour upon hour for this extraordinary piano circus have unfortunately not been recorded for posterity.

As the output of Brinsmead pianos grew, we find evidence of the firm time and again seeking ever-larger premises. The early, modest workrooms were in the Tottenham Court Road area (1837-*c*.1855), where there would have been a local pool of furniture-making expertise to be depended upon. Sizeable premises were eventually obtained in Chenies Street, Tottenham

The Brinsmead piano factory, Grafton Road, Kentish Town, 1874. [Illustration from The Pictorial World]

Court Road, during the late 1850s, by which date the firm was apparently producing between four and five hundred pianos per year, if the production serial numbers shown in *Pierce Piano Atlas* are accurate.[4] The Chenies Street premises in turn proved to be too small, and by 1874 an imposing, new purpose-built factory had been erected in Grafton Road, Kentish Town, close to Kentish Town West railway station. Business commuters travelling into the City via the North London Line would have had a grandstand view of Brinsmead production as their carriages traversed the railway viaduct overlooking the factory. They would have witnessed the daily spectacle of logs of timber going in at one end of the works – and highly-polished pianos emerging at the other.

The burgeoning output of the firm's instruments was due to the expansion of a thriving colonial market, which in turn had been aided by the remarkably-persuasive selling skills of Horace George Brinsmead. At one period during the early 1890s, Horace's selling talents had gained such a huge order book that the factory, embarrassingly, was totally unable to cope. As a result of Horace's international sales activities, the output of the firm doubled in a matter of a few years, and the Grafton Road factory had to be extended in size. Brinsmead pianos were certainly sought after globally. They must have been good.

For the first twenty-five years of its existence, the company had made only upright pianos – called either *cabinet pianos* if they were the taller variety, or *cottage pianos* if they were four feet or under in height. There had been no attempt to develop grand production, and there were understandable reasons for this: to embark upon grand construction requires considerable finance and a significantly greater manufacturing space than uprights; and of course the grand piano 'market' is a much more specialised and even a more risky area of the Trade when compared with the production of the ubiquitous upright instrument. For many years, John Brinsmead may not have had the spare capital, spare time, spare space, or even the required expertise, to consider grand production.

In February 1862, however, he designed and patented a new mechanism for the grand piano *having a perfect check, great power, and quick repetition.* There was only one slight problem: he was not actually building grand pianos at this date, and so he had no means of seeing his design come into fruition within a real working instrument. The way in which he surmounted this problem was extraordinary: he contacted Broadwoods, one of his rivals, and boldly asked them to provide him with one of their grands *minus an action*

A 'bellyman' busy in the Brinsmead factory, glueing on soundboard ribs by applying downward pressure with a series of vertical 'go bars'.

[Illustration from Joseph Hatton's article, 'How Pianos Are Made', from English Illustrated Magazine, 1892] *and keyboard.* Broadwoods may have been rather taken aback by such a highly-irregular request; but then they remembered how, a short time earlier, Brinsmead had actually done them a big favour – by lending them samples of his newly-designed threequarter iron-framed uprights in order for the details to be examined and, if necessary, copied.

And so on the 5th August 1862, a model 10 Broadwood rosewood boudoir grand (serial number 4583) left Broadwood's Horseferry Road workshops, Westminster, and was quietly delivered by horse and cart, under wraps, to Brinsmead's factory, unpolished, and without action and keys – for which a charge of £50 was made.[5] There is no doubt, therefore, that it was Broadwoods who made the first Brinsmead grand, although there is no evidence to show that they supplied Brinsmead with any more than one solitary instrument. Broadwoods must have been curious about John Brinsmead's patented new action. Perhaps they were hoping to be able to appropriate the new design for use in their own instruments, particularly as their own somewhat primitive 'single lever' grand action was receiving increasing criticism from professional concert pianists because of its heaviness.[6]

Shortly after a new Limited Company had been set up to manufacture Brinsmead instruments in the year 1899, it must have been with a real sense of disappointment that old John gradually realised that two of his sons would not succeed him in the family business. By the end of the year 1903, Tom and Horace had left the firm, and Edgar's worsening blindness increasingly prevented him from remaining an active participator (in fact, he died before his father, in 1907). From 1904, the general management of the firm was handed over to Brinsmead's grandson, Henry Billinghurst, the son of John's eldest daughter Rosa.[7] Although Billinghurst was a conscientious and hard-working administrator of the company, unfortunately he had little or no first-hand practical experience of piano making. As a result, he did not receive the same degree of loyalty from his Kentish Town piano makers as his Brinsmead uncles had done.

Thomas James Brinsmead (1844-1906), John's eldest son, was a practical piano maker and designer who ran the Grafton Road factory for many years. Following his withdrawal from the factory as a result of ill health in the late 1890s, he never rejoined the family firm, preferring instead to enter his wife's father's business, that of *J. & J. Goddard,* a flourishing piano supplies house based in Tottenham Court Road. Goddards was something of a mecca for London region piano tuners in the early 1900s, and it was a usual sight on

Thomas James Brinsmead (1844-1906).

[Photo: Rev. Keith Brinsmead]

Saturdays to see dozens of them arriving at the Tottenham Court Road shop in order to purchase their supplies of piano wire, tape ends, centre pins and sundry tools necessary for their routine work.[8] There, on many occasions, they might have met Tom Brinsmead, freed from his ties with his father's firm. In fact, the Brinsmead connection with Goddards was maintained for two further generations: Tom was succeeded as director by his son Herbert (Bertie) (1872-1954) and then by his grandson Keith (1906-1993), who later in life decided to quit pianos and become a vicar – as the Reverend Keith Brinsmead of Salisbury.

Tom Brinsmead's most notable contribution to the evolution of the piano is his invention of the *Top Tuner*, a completely new and novel way of tuning an upright instrument, which began to be manufactured by the company in the year 1881, its design protected by patent. In the Top Tuner model, the normal wooden wrestplank with horizontal tuning pins is replaced with *vertical* tuning pins which are machine threaded and pass through holes in a massive iron head bar at the top of the cast-iron frame. In order to tune the Top Tuner, a specially-made tuning key is required, which was usually supplied in a little leather pouch within the instrument. Tom's design was taken one stage further four year later, in 1885, when the Top Tuner model became 'backless'.[9] In this second design, which continued to incorporate the vertical pins, the usual wooden back bracings behind the soundboard are dispensed with, and the soundboard itself is attached to the instrument via screws in the cast-iron frame. This remarkable and even revolutionary 1885 design was in fact the forerunner of the many 'backless frame' models which began to appear on cheaper British upright pianos fifty years later.

On reflection, the Top Tuner model, although admirable in its novelty, was very fussy and expensive to manufacture, and as far as we are aware, the idea has never been taken up by other piano makers. The novelty of the tuning pin system might have helped sales on the showroom floor, but the high price asked for this particular model must have been some deterrent to sales. Tuning stability does not appear to have been particularly enhanced by Tom's invention. In fact, the main virtue of the design is the fact that the instrument is much more comfortable for the tuner's work when compared with the conventional upright. Nevertheless, the backless version of the 1885 Top Tuner is a highly original item of engineering, and confirms Tom Brinsmead's talent as an inventor.

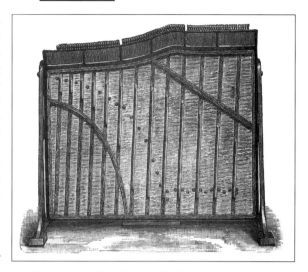

The Brinsmead Top Tuner in its final 'backless' version of 1885.

[Illustrations from History of the Pianoforte *by Edgar Brinsmead, 1889 edition]*

Edgar William Brinsmead (1848-1907), John's second son, was author of the book *History of the Pianoforte,* printed in vast quantities after its initial publication in the year 1868, when Edgar was only twenty years of age. Over the next twenty years, thirty thousand copies of the book were printed, a staggering quantity, which reflects

the enormous popularity of the piano at that period. It would also appear that copies of the book were sent (probably free of charge) to all Brinsmead agents throughout the English-speaking world, the idea being that happy purchasers of new Brinsmead instruments would receive the additional bonus of a complimentary copy of an attractively-produced hard-bound book.

Edgar William Brinsmead (1848-1907).
[Photo: Chris and Coral Brinsmead's archive]

Edgar's treatise has one unfortunate and embarrassing feature: its pages extol the virtues of the Brinsmead piano over and over again – particularly the 1889 edition, which comments more than a little favourably on the newly-introduced Top Tuner model. It is quite clear that the ultimate purpose of the book was to show the Brinsmead piano in a flattering light, in order to promote sales. This has led to the book's scornful dismissal by piano historians of more recent times. The most useful and valuable feature of Edgar's publication is in fact the appendix at the back, which painstakingly lists all the patents taken out for improvements in harpsichord and piano construction from the year 1694. Inevitably, the various Brinsmead patents (of dates 1862, 1868, 1871, 1875, 1879, 1881 and 1885) are particularly emphasised.

The youngest of the three Brinsmead brothers involved in the business, Horace George (1856-1908), went to sea on leaving school, but at the request of his family he left the merchant navy and entered the Grafton Road factory, where he learnt the skills of action finishing and regulating, as well as 'scale' design, the latter under the tuition of a Mr Rowe. As we noted earlier, Horace, whilst still in his twenties, had been pushed by his father to travel the world in order to represent the firm; but it seems clear that Horace, with his early seafaring experience, actually enjoyed the travel, and for a period he was happy to remain a resident in Australia with his wife, being involved in the work of tree planting there.

Following the formation of a Limited Company in 1899, Horace was re-called to London, appointed Brinsmead's managing director, and immediately began a thorough modernisation of the firm's fleet of instruments. In the course of one year, he introduced no fewer than ten new models, a remarkable achievement, which included a variety of overstrung grands of the

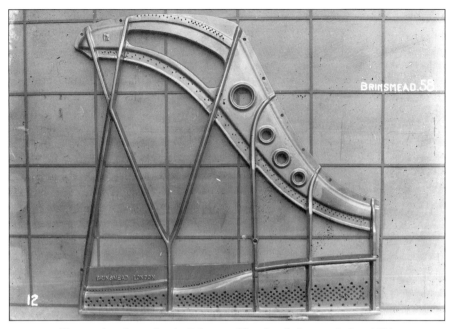

The cast-iron frame for the Brinsmead five-foot baby grand, circa 1900.

[Photo: Booth and Brookes ironfoundry archives, County Record Office, Colchester, Essex]

most up-to-date design, ranging in size from a 'baby' to a full-sized concert model. Horace's scale design knowledge, which he had learnt from Mr Rowe at the factory, must have been helpful in the creation of this new range of instruments.[10] Soon, however, there were problems for Horace: he had considerable disagreement with the new board of directors who had been introduced into the Limited Company, including Horace's own nephew, Henry Billinghurst. The generally unpleasant situation eventually led to Horace's decision to quit the family firm, which he did in November 1903. He then went on to form his own manufacturing concern in Great Marlborough Street, known as *Horace G. Brinsmead,* and began to make high quality, well-designed instruments in small numbers.

It was then that Horace began to experience severe misfortune: he was attacked by the original firm of John Brinsmead and Sons, who suggested to the piano-buying public that his pianos were not the 'genuine' article. As a result, Horace in 1906 seems to have lost most of his well-established export contacts in Australia. He experienced serious ill health as well, suffering a stroke; on top of all this, his diminishing sales and worrying finances were causes for serious concern; and his father, old John Brinsmead, who had been the bedrock of the family's piano-making interests, died in February 1908. Five months later, on the evening of the 21st July 1908, at his John Street warehouse off Tottenham Court Road, Horace shot himself in the heart with a revolver, so bringing his life to a tragic abrupt end, and leaving a wife and six young children to fend as best they could.[11]

At the outbreak of the First World War in 1914, almost one hundred of the Brinsmead workforce were recruited for active service. In the spring of 1917, the firm was obliged to turn over the majority of its activities to aircraft manufacture, and a new wood-converting mill was erected for this purpose. It was reported at the end of 1917 that as a result of the on-going military action, twelve Grafton Road employees had been killed, two were missing, sixteen were wounded, and one was a prisoner of war.[12] One of the curious outcomes of the War situation was Henry Billinghurst, the managing director's, intriguing plan to teach piano-making skills to British prisoners of war interned in Switzerland. His scheme involved bringing 'suitable prisoners' out of the camps at Mürren and Chateau d'Oex to premises on the northern shores of Lake Lucerne, there to commence classes in carpentry, joinery, cabinet-making, French polishing and piano making. By the end of 1917, some twenty prisoners were employed in the scheme, with plans to increase the number to eighty or more by April 1918.[13]

It had been a great shock to the British piano industry when the sad news of Horace Brinsmead's death was announced in 1908. It was an equal shock to the industry thirteen years later, when the firm of John Brinsmead and Sons Ltd was declared insolvent in the spring of 1921. There was a sale of bankrupt stock in May, the factory was closed in July, the company was wound up in September, and on the 17th October 1921 the name *John Brinsmead and Sons* and its goodwill (but not the company) was purchased by Walter Saville, director of the piano manufacturer and music publisher J. B. Cramer and Company.[14] The closure did not come as a shock to Henry Billinghurst, however: he knew that the family firm had been struggling financially for at least a decade; in fact as early as the year 1912 Henry had been contemplating the closure of the business. By the time the crunch finally came in 1921, he had made careful plans to wind down the firm in an orderly way, so that hardship to the shareholders and employees was reduced as much as possible.[15] As an example of this, arrangements were made for the apprentice tuner William Sale, whose indenture with Brinsmeads is dated the 20th May 1919, to be transferred to serve the remainder of his apprenticeship with the firm of Forrest & Sons of Shrewsbury on the 9th March 1920, a year before Brinsmead's closure.[16]

How this insolvency came about is fairly straightforward to analyse: there had been long-term financial difficulties, combined with new post-War problems, such as the acute shortage of raw materials and their very high cost, which made Brinsmead pianos expensive and difficult for the dealers to sell. In addition to this, the firm had experienced two prolonged strikes at the Grafton Road works, which decimated piano output and of course greatly reduced the financial turnover of the business. During the strikes, the only employees remaining were the small number of foremen (who were not in the Union), plus the young apprentices – who passed the time of day by having fun riding their bicycles up and down the deserted benchways.

Another reason given for the firm's failure was that the business had 'too many chiefs and not enough indians'. In other words, the firm was top heavy, with too large a management structure. At the factory, individuals carrying sheets of paper attached to clipboards were to be seen wandering around giving instructions, whilst fewer individuals were actually engaged in piano construction.

Following the sad closure of the Grafton Road works, Brinsmead production was transferred to Walter Saville's factory, conveniently sited only a stone's throw away in Castle Road, Kentish Town. We do not know how many former Brinsmead employees were taken on by Saville – probably only a handful of the most useful and qualified workers. The original Brinsmead designs were soon discontinued, and a completely new range of instruments introduced, the result of the design work of a senior Cramer employee, the appropriately-named William 'Bill' Scales. From 1921, the Brinsmead piano lost its separate identity, and was distinguishable from the Cramer instrument only by its nameplate. In other words, both brands shared exactly the same designs. In spite of this fact, the Brinsmead retailed at a higher price than the equivalent Cramer!

Walter Saville manufactured at Castle Road works no fewer than six sizes of grand piano, ranging from a tiny baby grand of only 4' 3" length to the largest concert model, nine feet in length. The two best grands, however, the seven-foot 'boudoir' and the nine foot 'concert', were reserved to be sold only with the name *Cramer* attached. Most of the retail piano sales appear to have taken place in shops actually owned by Saville, such as the chief showroom at 139 New Bond Street in the West End; in branches at Kensington, Notting Hill and in Moorgate in the City; and in regional music shops also owned by Saville, such as the retailers Harston and Son of Newark, Nottinghamshire.

In an unobtrusive way, Saville's multi-faceted firm was doing a great deal of business throughout the 1920s and '30s: piano manufacturing, retailing and music publishing. His firm's deliberate policy of cutting out the 'middle man' and selling largely through its own shops, helped to maintain profitability in difficult times for the piano industry during the inter-war years. A similar business policy was adopted by the old-established firm of Nathaniel Berry and Sons, which had its own factory at Crouch End making instruments exclusively for Berry's chain of music shops scattered throughout east London and south Essex.

Over the years, Walter Saville had collected a number of leading brand names and trademarks, such as *Justin Browne, Metzler* and *George Russell.* The acquisition of the *Brinsmead* name was a continuation of this policy. Pianos bearing all these trademarks were manufactured at Castle Road works. For example, by the year 1935 you could purchase in Saville's shops a model 'A' grand bearing the name 'Justin Browne', a model number 1 grand of the name 'Metzler', a baby grand made by 'George Russell', an XI grand being a highly-respectable 'Cramer' and, last but not least, the popular 'Midget' grand from the famous house of 'John Brinsmead and Sons'. All five grands were identical models (of 4' 3" length) and all of them were made in the same factory in Castle Road. The so-called 'genuine Brinsmead article' had now disappeared.

Output of pianos at Castle Road declined throughout the 1950s and '60s. Like Chappells during the same period, the production of Saville's pianos became very small, with only three or four instruments per week being produced by the dwindling workforce of the late 1950s. Nevertheless, it must have been an interesting factory to work in, embracing as it did so much rich north-London piano making tradition and knowledge.

Ultimately, a second generation of Savilles – two brothers – sold the whole business, apart from the retail shops and J. B. Cramer music publishing, to Kemble and Company in 1964, after which the manufacture of all Brinsmead and Cramer instruments was transferred to Kemble's own factory, then sited in Carysfort Road, Stoke Newington. Kemble and Company still retain ownership of the goodwill of the various Saville names, and, for example, have occasionally made a batch of Cramer pianos for the firm of Chui Pianos in Singapore.

One of the difficulties facing the piano historian when he or she tries to assess the importance of the Brinsmead piano is the problem of deciding how *good* Brinsmead instruments actually were. An influential writer on the subject, Cyril Ehrlich, was quite dismissive, and suggested that the firm was never more than an ordinary 'medium class' manufacturer.[17] On the other hand, the former Brinsmead apprentice William Sale (who has been mentioned earlier in this chapter) and who later worked for Bechstein in London, was adamant that there was very little difference between the best Brinsmead grands and similar grands by Bechstein.[18] It is hard to get to the truth, especially as there are very few original Brinsmead instruments still in first-class working order today.

From the evidence presented in this chapter, it is clear that the high watermark in the Brinsmead firm's success occurred during the closing decades of the 19th century. The company grew and prospered at this period as a result of a phenomenal increase in its 'colonial' trade, as well as a result of the steady growth of piano sales in Britain. The firm's impact on music making was clearly of far less importance in the 20th century, when Brinsmead's distinctive tonal identity was submerged among other brand names after the year 1921.

By the early 1970s, the Brinsmead piano had almost completely disappeared from piano shops. If pianos bearing the name were still being ordered from Kemble and Company, it was largely out of sentimental attachment to the name coming from a few dealers, rather than because of any distinctive musical or visual qualities the pianos might have had.

Today, very few pianists of the younger generation have even heard of the Brinsmead piano, although the name still commands a degree of respect from an elderly generation of piano lovers. There is still considerable interest in the old firm from descendants of John Brinsmead himself. These descendants are now scattered in all corners of the globe, but they enthusiastically communicate via a 'Brinsmead family' website. In view of the great deal of fascination and glamour surrounding this firm, and the need to save, repair, restore, study and analyse examples of the firm's best products (in particular the 'lost' concert grands), then there is perhaps the need for the establishment of a *Brinsmead Society* – to maintain and preserve the remnants and relics of this once-great Victorian enterprise.

2
CHALLEN

A NUMBER of years ago, the author of this book, dressed in shabby and tattered working clothes, was wandering aimlessly in a northern town. He came across the local piano shop – and decided to pay a visit. On entering the premises, he saw an interesting new upright with the name *Challen* attached. Underneath the name, in bold brass, was the inscribed lettering: *London 1804*. His curiosity aroused, he sat down at the instrument and began to strum. It made a good sound. Immediately, a young and worried-looking salesman appeared out of the blue and hissed wearily in the author's ear: 'Please, DON'T touch the pianos.' The humiliated author stood up, but had the satisfaction of rebuffing the salesman with the words: 'Do you know that this piano was NOT made in London, that Challen was NOT established in 1804, and do you know that I have recently been in correspondence with members of the Challen family?' In response, the salesman almost kicked the author out of the shop, and bluntly informed him that if he had any complaints, he should refer them to the manufacturer. That manufacturer probably lived in Malaysia.

Challen must be one of the best-known British marques. The name sounds elegant, and rolls off the tongue easily. During the 1930s, the well-capitalised and go-ahead Challen company secured a highly-prestigious contract for the supply of pianos to BBC studios. This connection was milked in the firm's advertising. 'Challen, the British Piano of the BBC' was an oft-heard expression at this date. The firm in its advertising promotions tried to cultivate a mystique of high quality; but as most tuners and technicians will know, the Challen has always been a medium-priced piano, with medium-quality components. Nevertheless, Challens are usually very well designed, and many of them have a fresh and pleasing tonal quality. In short, the company's instruments represented good value for money.

The firm was lucky to have had the services, at various times in its long history, of a number of outstanding 'scale' designers, such as Frank Challen, and his nephew, John Challen. We shall come across these individuals later on in this chapter; but before proceeding we must note one Challen instrument of outstanding design: the famous model '16' baby grand piano, in regular production from the early 1920s. From a design point of view, this was perhaps the best baby grand piano ever produced in Britain.

Looking into the roots of the company, we discover that the first of the line of piano makers was William Challen, who first appears in records as trading from 16, Clipston Street, Fitzroy Square, in the year 1835. This was over thirty years after the supposed founding date of the company (1804). For a few years up to 1835, however, Challen had been in partnership with a certain Alexander Watlen, and at least two instruments from this partnership (a square and a cabinet model) still survive.[19]

By the year 1838, Challen had moved to 41 Great Titchfield Street, where he had taken over the workshops of an old-established firm, Thomas Butcher, traceable at the same address back to the year 1811. London Post Office directories show that 'William Challen and Company' was based at the Great Titchfield Street address until 1859, after which the office and showrooms were transferred to prestigious premises at 3 Berners Street, Oxford Street.

There is an old legend within the piano trade which asserts that the Challen family became extremely wealthy as a result of piano manufacturing.[20] When an analysis is made of the firm's quite modest output for most of the second half of the nineteenth century (two or three hundred pianos per year during the period 1850-1865, rising to five hundred per year in the period 1865-1890) then this legend is hard to believe. The Census Return of 1861, however, shows that thirty-seven-year-old Charles Challen, William's son, by now a piano maker as well, was living in the company house above the Berners Street showrooms and actually employed a live-in governess for his three children's education, as well as two house servants. Here is evidence showing the Challen's reputed affluence.

Charles (born 1823) took over the business upon William's retirement in the year 1862. He had apparently received training as a piano maker in Bristol. From the year 1873, Charles in turn was joined in business by a third generation of the family: his elder son Charles Hollis Challen (1854-1921) and then a few years later by a younger son, Frank (1862-1919). Very few examples of nineteenth-century Challen instruments survive, and so it is quite hard for us to judge how good the firm's pianos were. The American piano historian Alfred Dolge, writing in the year 1911, described Challen models as 'excellent'.[21] In fact, already by the year 1863 the company had been awarded a prize medal (donor unknown) for 'excellent action and tone'.

We are not really sure where the original Challen workshops were sited, but we know that they were close to Euston railway station, and at a later date moved a mile or so north to Camden Town. There is a curious account of the origins of Challen's later factory in the book *Memories of Sixty Years in the Timber and Pianoforte Trades,* written by Louis Bamberger and published around the year 1930:

> *Henry Ward* [a piano maker] *built a large factory in Arlington Road, Camden Town and occupied it for some years. Later on, he built another factory adjoining, so as to oblige his old friend Charles Challen, whose factory close to Euston station had been acquired for street improvements.*

Bamberger gives no date for this event, but the idea of any piano maker providing a second factory next door to his own in order to house a competitor in the same field seems rather a strange one! The Challen works remained in Arlington Road until 1914. Then the firm moved into premises in nearby Archer Street (now called Curnock Street) which had recently been vacated by the well-known firm of piano makers, George Rogers and Sons.

Of the two Challen brothers just mentioned, Charles Hollis became the commercial director of the firm (in fact, the company was eventually named after him: *Charles H. Challen and Company Ltd*). Frank's role was much more of a technical nature: he managed the factory, where he had learnt all aspects of construction. Frank soon became well known in the Trade as a gifted designer, and by the early 20th century his fame had spread, so that he was generally regarded as being 'the best scale designer in the trade'.[22] In the year 1907, following a serious and unfortunate dispute with his elder brother, he quit the family business and took on the job of factory manager and designer at J. and J. Hopkinson Ltd, of Fitzroy Road, Primrose Hill, a firm producing pianos of similar quality to Challens. Hopkinson's old factory building still survives in Fitzroy Road, although it hasn't seen a piano since the late 1930s. The building has an interesting 'gothic revival' facade, incongruously sandwiched in the middle of a row of terraced houses.

Once he was settled in his new job, Frank Challen set to work designing a range of better Hopkinson instruments – which became the talk of the Trade because of their excellent music qualities. The Hopkinson uprights were modelled on the best contemporary German designs. When Frank took his instruments to the international Fairs at Brussels (1910) and Turin (1911) his large and sonorous model 12 upright won the Grand Prix medal on both occasions. After the Hopkinson company amalgamated with that of George Rogers and Sons, it is highly likely that Frank's designs were used for Rogers instruments as well.

Frank Challen (1862-1919).
[Photo: Katherine Challen]

His great interest in piano design and construction made Frank acutely aware of the total absence of theoretical and design training for young apprentices within the industry. As secretary to the Piano Manufacturers' Association in 1911, he tried to persuade his fellow makers to sponsor the founding of a 'Trade School' in which skills such as piano design could be learned; but the idea met with very poor response, apart from one or two individuals such as Lionel Shenstone the keyboard maker. Undaunted by the indifference of the trade to a crying need for technical training, Frank single-handedly negotiated with the education authorities to establish a suitable training centre. The fruits of his efforts came in 1913 with the commencement of evening classes (later, day release classes). After the First World War, these same classes were based at the Northern Polytechnic in Holloway Road, and the first technical lecturers were Samuel Wolfenden (himself a former designer for the Rogers company) and Sydney A. Hurren. Between them they educated a new generation of young piano technicians in the art of piano design and construction, Samuel Wolfenden going on to write two valuable books about the subject.[23]

Young students at the Northern Polytechnic, Holloway Road, London, learning the practical skill of upright action finishing, **circa 1930.**

[Photo: Author's collection]

The piano technology classes founded by Frank Challen have continued, in various forms, to the present day. From the 1960s, they were based at the London College of Furniture in Pitfield Street, Hoxton. They moved with the College in 1970 to new premises at 41 Commercial Road, where a small piano technology course with about a dozen students continues, now administered by the London Metropolitan University. Unfortunately, as a result of recent financial cutbacks (2009) the future of this course looks very unsure, in spite of the fact that it has provided a valuable training ground for almost one hundred years.

During the First World War, which brought London piano manufacture almost to a standstill, Frank Challen kept himself occupied creating a range of new designs which were to be generally available for the Trade to use, in order to help 'get the industry back on its feet' (as Frank put it) after hostilities had ceased. Sadly, Frank's eldest son Christopher, also a trained piano maker, died of War wounds in 1918, and this tragedy helped to lead to a breakdown in Frank's own health. He died in July 1919 at the comparatively young age of fifty-six.

As a personality, Frank Challen was modest and retiring, a charming dreamer, and not a hard-headed business man. He was perhaps something of a misfit among many of the hard-bitten piano makers of Camden Town, who would not have appreciated his idealism. His daughter, the late Miss Katherine Challen, wrote to the author when she was very elderly, in August 1983, with the following interesting information about her father:

> *I think he was very much a man's man – very keenly interested in the Highgate Debating Society and not personally involved with his family like some modern fathers are. He was a great reader and buyer of books, and we all benefited from that. Nobody in [their branch of] the Challen family was particularly expert musically, although four of us had music lessons. My mother belonged to the Royal Choral Society, which then met at Queens Hall, and my father had a pleasant singing voice when they sang duets. My father was a great walker at weekends. He loved the Sussex Downs from which the Challens came – Storrington and Steyning were favourite places. No doubt our love of walking comes from him.*

It was during the First War period that the Challen company became well known for producing a small grand of good design and at a reasonable price. In fact, at one point in its history, the firm seriously considered turning over the whole of its factory production exclusively for the manufacture of such small instruments. We do not know whether the design of the earliest of these baby grands was the work of Frank before he left the company in 1907, or whether in fact most of the scaling and design work was done by his nephew, John Duff Challen (1888-1947) who succeeded his uncle as technical director. If Frank *had* been the designer of the earlier models, then John Challen without doubt played a role in the evolution of the firm's later small grands, such as the model 16, which reached its final form with a seven and one quarter octave compass in the early 1920s.

John Challen (1888-1947).
[Photo: Margaret Wolfe-Barry]

John Challen's daughter, Margaret, remembers her father carrying out a considerable proportion of his routine design work at their family home. She remembers his drawing office there, with rolls and rolls of huge sheets of paper spread everywhere in sight; and she would see her father bent over his work in a highly concentrated manner. When he wasn't drafting out a new scale design, her father would spend hours at the piano, going through the classical repertoire. He was certainly an accomplished pianist.[24]

Perhaps we should dwell on some of the features of the Challen 16 grand for some moments. This little musical creation is exactly five feet (152cm) long. Tuners and technicians who are familiar with the instrument will confirm that the frame design possesses elegance and simplicity. One of its superficial features, which aids identification of the model, is a solitary, round hole in the iron hitch plate at the instrument's bentside. Another distinctive feature is the character of the outer case construction at the junction of treble cheek and curved rim. On the case of the model 16, and all subsequent grands of Challen manufacture, this junction has a visually-pleasing pointed 'corner', as distinct from the comparatively nebulous continuous curve (the result of a continuous laminated rim) found in the modern Steinway or Yamaha. In fact, the 'Challen corner' has sadly disappeared as a case feature on all modern grands, apart from the Viennese-made Bosendorfer, and then only in the larger and more 'old fashioned'-looking models by this illustrious maker.

Although the '16' is only five feet long, it possesses acceptable string lengths in those two 'difficult' areas of small piano construction: the tenor end of the mainbridge (longest string length here, 101cm) and the lowest bass strings (bottom A is 111cm in length). The top twenty-five notes in the high treble press against a 'capo d'astro' bearing bar, an integral part of the iron frame, whilst the middle and treble sections are fitted with brass bearing studs. A considerable proportion of model 16s turn up with the name *John Broadwood & Sons* attached. This phenomenon will be explained later on in this chapter.

One of the attractive features of Challen's baby grands was their very reasonable cost. Dealers could buy one from the factory at around £60 trade price in the period 1910-1916. The purchase records of Wigmore Hall Piano Galleries, which survive for the fifty-year period between 1916 and 1966, show that the retail company was buying in about one small Challen grand each month during the period 1916-1918. In the latter year, there was an unprecedented increase in the price of all London-made instruments, largely as a

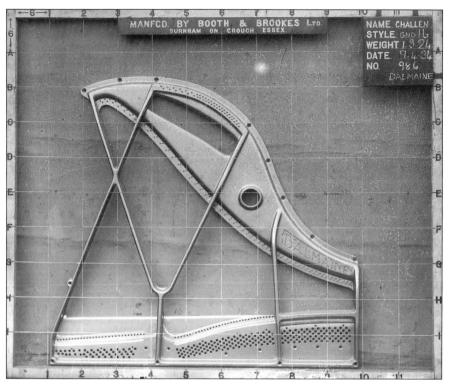

**The cast-iron frame for the famous model 16 Challen baby grand,
photographed in 1934.**

[Photo: Booth and Brookes ironfoundry archives, County Record Office, Colchester, Essex]

result of the post-War scarcity of raw materials. By the end of 1918, the Challen baby grand cost £103 trade. By July 1919, a further unavoidable increase in raw material costs meant that the same instrument was now priced at £112, a doubling over a three-year period. By the end of 1919 the cost of the instrument had reached the staggering price of £138 trade, and Wigmore Hall Galleries responded by simply cancelling orders for further Challen models.[25]

Then in July 1920, the first of the Petrof grands began to be imported from Czechoslovakia, and Wigmore Galleries went in for bulk purchasing. In 1921, for instance, the firm bought in forty Petrof instruments of various kinds, and, presumably as a result of the bulk purchase, was able to obtain a small Petrof grand in black polish for only £84 trade, which hugely undercut the price of the equivalent Challen. To make matters worse, Bosendorfer of Vienna began to send instruments to England from June 1922, and the very desirable Bosendorfer 5' 6" grand, arguably a tonally-superior instrument to the Challen, could be obtained by Wigmore Galleries for only £93 trade. In the light of this situation, it seems remarkable that Charles H. Challen and Company managed to survive at all. In 1922, the firm was certainly ailing, apparently producing only just over one hundred instruments in that year; [26] and John Challen would have doubtless noted the depressing evidence of shrinking production from other well-established London piano factories. Although output had risen somewhat by the mid 1920s, the Archer Street factory appeared unable to produce more than about five hundred pianos each year (about ten each week) until 1928.

During the decade from 1928 to 1938, however, Challen's production increased dramatically: by 1937, the number of instruments made (some 3,000 in that year) represented a six-fold increase on the levels of output during the 1920s. The reason was this: a major shareholding in the company had been purchased around the year 1927 by an ambitious and highly capable businessman, Willie Evans, who then became a director and virtual owner of the firm. His directorship was linked to his massive injection of capital into the business, enabling a huge growth in piano output.

Willie Evans, CBE.

[Photo: John Broadwood & Sons Ltd]

We know very little about Evans' origins, other than the fact that he was a Welshman, that he was actually baptised 'Willie' as a baby, and that he was the son of a police inspector. He came to London as a young man, seeking work as a skilled engineer, and in the early 1920s found employment at the factory belonging to the Chappell Piano Company in Ferdinand Street, Chalk Farm. Evans held the post of works engineer, a position which involved such tasks as the construction of specialist manufacturing equipment (jigs and templates) and the maintenance of wood-finishing machinery. He had no previous experience with pianos, but he was very enthusiastic, and he managed to persuade the Chappell management to allow him to tinker with the existing iron frame of the firm's well-established five-foot *Elysian* grand. His experiment, in February 1924, which involved removing some of the iron bars at the cross-over point in the overstrung scale, in order to make the grand look somewhat 'barless', was a terrible disaster. According to a former Chappell tuner working in the factory at the time, the experiment 'almost ruined the company.'[27] Willie Evans left Chappells shortly afterwards – obviously under a cloud – and his dalliance with piano design seemed to be over.

It was then that he came into some very good luck: he met the woman who was to become his wife. Not only was Dilys beautiful, she was extremely rich as well – she was an heiress. She very kindly provided Evans with a comfortable home and a large amount of cash with which to buy into the Challen company. Following Evans' investment, John Challen lost control of the family business. Speaking at the Leeds Publicity Club in late 1934, Willie Evans was able to declare:

> *When I took over the derelict business about eight years ago, I found only one order on the firm's books, about a dozen apprentices in the factory, and an army of cockcroaches on the premises.*[28]

He could rightfully boast that by 1929 he had 'turned round' the ailing Challen business, doubling the piano output in the course of one year. His bold and fearless plans led him to uproot the Challen workforce from Archer Street in the spring of 1932, and place them in a newly-constructed well-lit factory at The Hyde, Hendon, Middlesex. Evans, with his engineering and tooling skills, reorganised production, so that manufacturing in the new factory was more efficient than it had been in Archer Street. This enabled the Challen grand to be reduced in price, which, of course, helped sales enormously. Remarkably, Evans was able to get the price of the 16 grand down to £60 trade, close to the price it had been before 1918. As an example of the way in which this was done, we can note that the model 16 had previously been constructed with an underlying braced back comprising numerous wooden posts. Under Evans, it was now made in a quicker and more simplified way by using a special jig to rapidly create a single-piece laminated 'belt', around which the case rim could be built. The rapidly increasing numbers of pianos made, as a result of Mrs Evans' input of capital, obviously played a significant role in bringing down the unit costs as well. Components could now be purchased in much larger quantities, which substantially reduced their price.

Challen's piano factory, 32-44 Archer Street (now Curnock Street), Camden Town.
The premises are now demolished.

[Photo: Camden Local Studies Library, Holborn, London]

Among the workers who moved from Archer Street to Hendon was a young lad, Leslie Lawrence (1910-1972) who had just left school in order to begin an apprenticeship as an upright action finisher. During his apprenticeship, Lawrence was sent to the Northern Polytechnic, Holloway Road, on those day-release classes which had been established by Frank Challen some years earlier. On his arrival at the Polytechnic, Lawrence was taught by Sydney Hurren, who soon recognised that the young apprentice had a special aptitude and talent for scale drawing and design. Hurren was keen to impart this obscure skill, and Lawrence became his star pupil. One day, on his return to the factory, Leslie was taken into the office and casually informed by Evans that instead of installing actions and keyboards into upright pianos, he was now going to take on the far more important role of designer of new grand and upright pianos for the firm. Young Lawrence gulped – he was only in his early twenties, and he must have been quite bewildered; but he rose to the challenge, and no doubt with valuable help from Hurren behind the scenes, he created over the next few years an interesting variety of new models, some of which are outstanding tonally.

The well-established '16' appears to have been the only grand in regular production when Willie Evans took over the firm. It is therefore understandable that he would be anxious to widen the product range. After Lawrence began his work, the '16' was joined by six new sister grand models of lengths 4 foot, 4' 3", 4' 6", 6' 4", 8 feet, and even 10 feet long. No fewer than *seven* grand rim-bending presses were soon to be seen on the floor of the Hendon factory, and so it is easy to see how Mrs Evans' welcome capital had been utilised. Some of the presses could produce the rims for two different models; for example, the press for the 4 foot 6 inch model was also used to make a special 'double overstrung' version of the same-sized instrument. We are certainly impressed when we learn that Lawrence created all these new instruments before he had reached the age of twenty-six.

In March 1931, an event occurred which was to be of enormous benefit to the Challen company: the old-established London firm of John Broadwood and Sons Ltd ran into serious financial difficulties and lost its factory at Stour Road, Hackney. The skilled Broadwood workforce was dismissed, the stock of materials was sold off, and even the various jigs, patterns and templates necessary for manufacture appeared to have been destroyed following the insolvency.[29] The Broadwood company managed to survive only in name, and with a piano tuning connection as the only means of generating income left, it obviously needed to find an alternative source of new instruments. Evans was approached. He was busy developing his new grand models, but

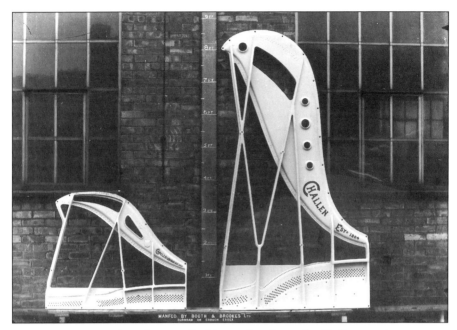

Largest and smallest: two freshly-cast iron frames for Challen grands, standing outside Booth and Brookes ironfoundry, Burnham-on-Crouch, Essex, early 1930s. The small frame on the left is for the 4' 6" baby; the huge frame on the right is for the 10-foot concert instrument.

[Photo: Booth and Brookes ironfoundry archive, Essex Record Office, Chelmsford]

with typical boldness he enthusiastically agreed to shoulder the responsibility and take on the manufacture of instruments for Broadwood. He was even willing to take on a contingent of around twenty former Broadwood employees, which was of course a valuable input of much-needed skill if production was to be expanded.

All of the Challen designs were then made ready for Broadwood's use. This explains why so many of the '16' grands from the 1930s show up with the 'Broadwood' name attached. The manufacturing agreement between the two firms was to remain in place until the outbreak of the Second World War in 1939. From 1945, Broadwoods re-established their own factory.

In the year of King George V's Silver Jubilee (1935), Willie Evans proudly announced that the Challen company was going to commemorate the event by building the 'largest grand piano in the world', a giant specimen having the slightly preposterous length of almost twelve feet. Evans was perhaps angling for a 'Royal Warrant', particularly as his firm was already making considerable quantities of instruments for Broadwoods, the Warrant holders. Leslie Lawrence then busied himself at what must have been the longest drawing board in the world. In a short time, a wooden master pattern had been created at the iron foundry of Booth and Brookes Ltd, situated at Burnham-on-Crouch in Essex. The first enormous casting was delivered from Burnham to Hendon, installed in the prototype, and then strung up; but alas! The iron frame cracked with an almighty explosion just as soon as the string tension was applied. The workforce was dismayed: but Evans was undeterred. He boldly ordered another casting from the foundry. Everyone at Challens must have been highly apprehensive of what might happen at this second attempt at a world record. This time, the frame did not crack, nor did other ones of slightly later date.

A sigh of relief was breathed at Hendon, but we shall never know whether the King was impressed by Evans' efforts; he certainly did not place an order for a specimen of this exceptional instrument. The prototype of the 'monster' was displayed at the British Industries Fair of 1935, and when the Fair was visited by Queen Mary, the grand was demonstrated to her by the famous

'The Largest Grand Piano in the World', 1935.
Seated proudly at the keyboard is the piano's designer, Leslie Lawrence.
His older brother Albert, a Challen tuner, listens, impressed.
[Photo: Bill Kibby, Piano History Centre, Great Yarmouth]

light-music pianist and composer, Billy Mayerl. Following the Fair, the largest grand piano in the world was moved into a BBC studio and broadcast to the nation.

By the summer of 1936, Leslie Lawrence had completed his range of new models as requested. He suddenly found himself with nothing much to do. He twiddled his thumbs for some days, and then went to Evans for advice. In response, Evans told him that he must return to installing upright actions again, as there was no other work for him to do. This made Lawrence resentful; he felt humiliated and undervalued, and shortly afterwards left the company – although he was in fact willing to rejoin the firm again for a period shortly after the Second World War. Perhaps his best model, from a musical point of view, is his 6' 4" grand (the model 19). Although this instrument was made in a simple and inexpensive way, it possesses a highly satisfactory, fresh tonal quality – in fact, the model has a far more characterful and interesting sound than many of the grands which are made in the Far East today. It makes it all the more depressing when one learns that the special tooling for this particular instrument was thoughtlessly broken up in 1970. To replace such manufacturing items with new today would cost something in the region of £70,000 – just for the one model.

It was the '19' which was chosen in 1936 by the BBC (following a sound test behind screens, so that the make of instrument could not be identified). It became the main 'workhorse' for use in broadcasting and recording sessions over the next thirty years. By the mid 1950s, over one hundred model 19s were in regular use in various studios up and down the country, being regularly serviced by Challen factory technicians.

It must have been a wonderful contract to have had. The mid 1930s were certainly exciting and glamorous times for Challen, under Willie Evans' inspired leadership. For his services to piano making, Evans was awarded the CBE. It is hard for us to realise today what a tremendous honour, and a tremendous bonus, the BBC contract must have been for the company. Sales of Challen instruments increased even further as the general public became aware of the BBC connection. In 1937, the year of its greatest level of production, the firm manufactured 3,085 new pianos.[30] But from the early 1960s, the BBC seemed to prefer Steinway. By that date, anyway, the Challen company, under new management, had lost interest in the making of larger, higher-quality grands, and the directors appeared to let the valuable BBC connection slip between their fingers.

Broadcasting to the Nation: a Challen grand in use at a BBC radio studio, Birmingham, mid 1930s.

[Photo: Author's collection]

With the Second World War came the closure of the Hendon factory, along with most other London piano factories. The Hendon works were never to open again for piano production, and by the early 1950s, Challen had become based at the smaller *Omega Works* in Hermitage Road, Harringay. Mr Leslie Pearce, a well-known London-based grand piano technician, was working at Challens around this date, and he remembers some of the personalities who made up the grand production team. There was the eccentric Horace Prior, a grand case constructor, who had originally worked for Broadwoods, and who formed part of the group joining Challens when Broadwood's works closed down in 1931. Prior was an unashamed meths drinker, and was famous for his lurid red nose and also for his battered bowler hat, which he wore throughout the working day, summer or winter. Another highly-skilled technician was James 'Jimmy' Gibbs, a grand action finisher. Gibbs had been trained at Chappells, and was noted for his meticulous workmanship of the highest order. Only he was allowed to undertake the final finishing and regulation of Challen's best grands, such as the model 19 and others destined for the BBC.

The grand production team in the early 1950s seems to have been based on groups of two workers: there were two 'markers off', two rim laminators, a couple of fitters up (Horace Prior, one other, and apprentices); and then there was a team of four or five action finishers, who installed the action and keyboards into each instrument and then proceeded with necessary regulation of the action mechanism. Grand finishers are usually the 'blue-eyed boys' in a piano factory situation: they are easily the most skilled individuals, and usually the highest paid, within the workforce. Challen's grand finishers in the early 1950s included Ted Wicking, Wally Gurden and Alf Jacobs, as well as Jimmy Gibbs and Les Pearce.

According to Les Pearce, the output of grands at this date would be around twelve instruments per month. The foreman of grand finishing for many years was Ted Wicking, who eventually became factory manager at the Omega Works, following the death of Fred Oliver. By the early 1970s, Ted had left Challens and was giving valuable service working as a lecturer in piano technology at the London College of Furniture (later called the London Metropolitan University) in Commercial Road. His kind-heartedness and helpfulness towards many young students is well remembered.

Willie Evans remained head of the Challen firm throughout the 1950s, but towards the end of that decade he became seriously ill, and so he quickly decided to sell his business and retire to Poole in Dorset. He was to enjoy some twenty years of retirement before his death on the 15th July 1980. Both Evans and his wife Dilys were very religious, and as they had no children of their own, their fortune of some £400,000 was bequeathed to charitable causes, such as the British and Foreign Bible Society, the Scripture Union, and the London City Mission.[31]

In 1959, Evans sold his business to Brasted Brothers Ltd, whose factory, by coincidence, was close by, further along Hermitage Road. Production trundled a few hundred yards down the road, and Challen workers were placed in new surroundings. The take-over by Brasted was never seen as a particularly good move within the industry. Brasted Brothers concentrated on volume output of small, cheap pianos, such as the popular and affordable 'Eavestaff Minipiano'. The firm had achieved great success in the sales of this attractive, compact little instrument from the mid 1930s; but Brasteds were always anxious to build pianos down to a price. It is hard to see how the up-market aspect of the Challen business could possibly flourish in this situation. In fact, Challen grand production withered. There appears to have been little or no real interest in training young employees in the necessary skills of grand piano making. The friendly Brasted family who ran the firm were highly-skilled in marketing and accounts, but they were never ever seen with their shirt sleeves rolled up on the shop floor, trying to discover what it was that made good piano tone.[32]

By the late 1960s, visitors to the Hermitage Road factory would have found just one grand finisher at work, the elderly and distinguished-looking Alf Jacobs. What little grand production there was had become largely concentrated on the smaller, cheaper and musically inferior models, such as the '29', of only four-foot length. Output of the larger, quality grands had fossilised. Then in 1970, a surprise announcement was made to the Trade: Brasted Brothers Ltd was going to close down, and all the various Challen designs – plus the Challen goodwill – were going to be purchased by Barratt and Robinson Ltd, whose factory actually adjoined that of Brasteds in Hermitage Road.

If the take-over of Challen by Brasted in 1959 had not been particularly good news, then the acquisition by Barratt and Robinson in 1970 was even worse. B & R prided itself on making the cheapest possible instruments in the Trade. Challen plunged down market. Within a few months the Challen instrument lost its identity almost entirely, and the brand name was cheerfully attached to a bewildering range of undistinguished budget instruments of all shapes and sizes.

Amazingly, production of a few grands lingered on, largely as a result of the input of the elderly Ron Howkins, a highly-skilled and versatile craftsman, who single-handedly carried out many of the construction processes, from bellying and marking off, to casework fitting up. It was only as a result of his presence in the B & R factory that there was any grand production at all. Only two sizes of grand continued to be produced: the '16' and the '29'. All the larger 'professional' models of the type supplied to BBC studios were discontinued after 1970, and their rim-bending bucks broken up. Ron Howkins led something of a double life: by day he was a grand piano constructor; by night, he and his wife Vi were noted national ballroom dancing champions!

The early 1980s were difficult times for British piano manufacturing. The once-vigorous home-based manufacturing was in trouble as a result of successful competition from instruments made in the Far East, such as Yamaha, Kawai, Samick and Young Chang. As far as price and quality were concerned, London makers found it increasingly difficult to compete. Sadly,

MODELS 29 & 16

4 ft. (122 cm.) & 5 ft. (152 cm.)
LONG RESPECTIVELY
BOTH 7¼ OCTAVES

THESE, OUR DOMESTIC GRAND PIANOS, ARE BOTH HIGHLY COMMENDABLE, MUSICAL QUALITY BEING PROPORTIONATE TO SIZE

THE BRITISH PIANO OF THE B.B.C.

The Challen '16' grand, in a figured walnut case.

[Illustration from a Challen publicity brochure, circa 1960]

by 1984 we had almost stopped making grands in this country, apart from an occasional six-foot Welmar, finished in the Blüthner Perivale workshops. Over a span of four years, between 1980 and 1984, a number of important London factories closed down: Broadwood (Acton), Danemann (Islington) Zender (Hackney), and Rogers (Tottenham). In 1984, Barratt and Robinson Ltd became insolvent and was placed in the hands of the official receiver, Mr J. Alexander of accountants Thomson McLintock and Company, who took measures to close the factory and wind-up the concern.

It was then that certain 'manufacturing items' belonging to B & R were offered for sale. The author of this book became very curious when he learnt that the wherewithal to make the renowned Challen 16 was among the items included. He visited the now-deserted factory, and on entering the main production shop saw a never-to-be-forgotten sight: what appeared to be a huge pile of broken-down driftwood and scrap metal lying in a heap on the floor. Were these bits and pieces indeed the wherewithal to make the '16', the very last Challen grand in production? Yes they were. A purchase price was agreed, and the various items were transported to the author's own piano-building workshop at Otley in West Yorkshire.

It was soon discovered, however, that a number of important ingredients in the kit – small but essential jigs and templates – were unfortunately missing; and of course that most essential item, the full-size scale drawing itself, showing the layout of the strings, had been long lost. 'Piano makers DON'T use drawings', asserted a former director of B & R when enquiries were made. 'They just use little bits and pieces of wood as templates.' When one reflects on this statement, it makes one believe that sections of the British piano-manufacturing industry actually deserved to perish in the early 1980s. But the director was right in his assertion, as we shall shortly see.

Luckily, the author was able to make contact with the very elderly and very amiable Ron Howkins, the last-known person to have 'shop floor' knowledge of Challen 16 production. Although he was seriously ill in hospital and first wrote to the author from his hospital bed, Ron very kindly agreed to risk the long trek northwards to Otley, and a few weeks later, his health improved, he staggered into the piano workshops of *Laurence & Nash* accompanied by his wife Vi. 'Where is that stick of rosewood about twenty inches long with a deep notch carved at one third of its length?' enquired Ron anxiously. Like other vital ingredients in the '16' kit, it was missing. 'Then you are in big trouble' said Ron, gasping for breath.

Nevertheless, in spite of this setback (the stick in question was used to indicate the critical distance between soundboard headbar and front of the keybottom) Ron Howkins did take great pains to explain verbally how he actually put together the model 16, and all this information was carefully written down. Being told about the significance of one little nail which stuck out at the side of the rim-bending press was all part of this initiation. One example of the 16 grand – and one only – was completed in Yorkshire before the Otley workshop sadly closed down in August 1989. Shortly afterwards, the contents of the grand manufacturing kit were sold to Ken Forrest, a highly knowledgeable technician with a workshop at Colne, Lancashire. It was Ken's wish to continue with the manufacture of the '16'; but he was in such demand as a concert tuner throughout Yorkshire at this period that he never had sufficient time to take things further, and the kit stood in a corner of his workshop, gathering dust.

Sixteen years went by. Then in 2007 the author approached Ken Forrest and offered to re-purchase the items in question. The offer was accepted, and so all the various bits and pieces were uprooted yet again and transported back to the south of England – this time to outbuildings at Finchcocks Museum, at Goudhurst, Kent. Since the summer of 2007, the items needed to manufacture the '16', including the two rim presses, have been on public display as part of a 'working museum' of piano-making ephemera. The display has been seen by many curious visitors to Finchcocks. Most of the '16' tackle has been restored, and is in full working order. This means that at some future date, there is the possibility of an enthusiast using the items to re-commence grand manufacture. But of course they will not be allowed to use the name 'Challen' on any new instrument: this trademark now belongs to a firm called Musical Products, of Malaysia, who are busy distributing a range of new Chinese Challens for import into Europe.[33]

3
COLLARD & COLLARD

THE names *Collard and Collard* were once household words, as well known in the nineteenth century as the brand names 'Coca Cola' and 'Hoover' were in the twentieth. The reason for this stems from the fact that the Collard firm was for many years the largest piano manufacturer in England, and during the later decades of the nineteenth century the firm built up a network of global customers throughout the British Empire. It is estimated that from the 1860s onwards, a steady stream of at least forty pianos per week poured out of Collard's London factory.[34]

There used to be a well-known music hall joke used by stand-up comics, which went something like this:

> 1st Comedian: *I say, I say, I say! Did you hear that two bailiffs visited my next-door neighbour and forcibly took away the piano?*
>
> 2nd Comedian: *So they've got your neighbours collared at last?*
>
> 1st Comedian: *You mean their Collard and Collard?*

The identities of the two founding partners have sometimes been confused. The individuals concerned were two brothers, Frederick William Collard (1772-1860) and his younger brother, William Frederick (1776-1866), both of whom hailed from the rural Somerset village of Wiveliscombe, which they had left by the 1790s in order to work in London. The close

Frederick William Collard (1772-1860).
[Portrait: John Collard's archive]

similarity of the two brothers' names has certainly led to confusion. Matters are not helped by the fact that their older sister, Phoebe Collard (1764-1855) married *another* William Collard (her cousin), and it was Phoebe's two sons, Frederick William and Charles Lukey Collard, who eventually succeeded their uncles in the piano-manufacturing business. At one point in the mid nineteenth century, a visitor to the firm requesting to speak to a 'Mr Collard' might have been asked: 'Do you mean Mr Frederick William, Mr William Frederick, the other Mr William, or Mr Frederick William junior?' It is easy to see how confusion arose.

The senior founding partner, Frederick, arrived in London around the year 1789, when he was aged 17. He found employment, possibly as an apprentice, at the City of London music publishers, music sellers and musical instrument dealers, *Longman & Broderip,* trading at the sign of the Harp and Crown, 26 Cheapside. Young Collard as shop boy lived above the retail premises. In our imagination we can see him dutifully opening up the place early each working day, and sweeping the floor. As an old man, Frederick reflected on the remarkable fact that he had continuously lived 'over the shop' for no less than seventy years.[35]

It must have been a fascinating place in which to have lived and worked. Longman and Broderip's music store provided a wide variety of items, ranging from sheet music, music stands and tuning forks, to grand and square pianos, guitars and flutes. It was a music-selling emporium, with enthusiastic musically-inclined customers arriving through the door from all parts of the country. In addition to publishing music, the firm was involved to some extent in manufacturing. It had its own keyboard instrument workshops in Tottenham Court Road by the 1790s, for example, although a great deal of the instruments sold in the shop were actually constructed by self-employed contracted 'outworkers', such as Thomas Culliford, who occupied workshops in Fountain Court to the rear of the Cheapside premises.[36] Invariably, all the musical instruments on display in the Cheapside shop bore the trademark *Longman & Broderip.*

On the 30th November 1799, Frederick Collard married Mary Lukey. She was the daughter of a certain Charles Lukey, a former partner in the firm of Longman and Broderip. Charles had died at a relatively young age in 1776, sadly when Mary was only about two years old. It seems likely that the Lukeys had kept in touch with the Cheapside business, however, enabling Frederick to meet Mary on many occasions. For an outline tree of the Collards, which helps to explain the complicated family kinship, the reader is referred to Appendix 4 in this book.

Longman and Broderip ran into serious financial difficulties in the mid-1790s, largely as a result of the over-borrowing of the senior partner, James Longman. The firm was declared bankrupt in 1795, and Longman ended up in the debtor's prison.[37] From 1798, however, things began to improve when a consortium of six equal partners took over the business, led by the eminent composer and pianist Muzio Clementi (1752-1832). New capital was found. One of the six investors was twenty-six-year-old Frederick Collard, by now an employee of almost ten years' standing. We wonder how Collard managed to acquire the necessary capital at such a young age. Clementi, who was a shrewd and capable man of business, became the 'figurehead' of the firm. He must have often gathered a delighted audience of shoppers when he demonstrated keyboard instruments in the Cheapside showroom.

In order to distance itself from Longman, and to acknowledge the arrival of the famous composer as a partner, the name of the firm was changed to *Clementi and Company,* with its headquarters remaining at the original Cheapside address. During the course of his business travels for the firm, on the continent in the early 1800s, Muzio Clementi corresponded regularly with the young Frederick Collard, on one occasion reminding him of the need to ensure that the firm's instruments were as good as those made by Broadwood, their chief competitor. 'You have a good ear; compare,' he wrote to Collard from Dresden in August 1803.[38] This small shred of evidence suggests that Frederick was very much involved in the practical side of piano making, probably overseeing the final tuning, voicing and regulation of the new instruments in the Cheapside shop.

Today, when a *circa* 1800 grand made by the Clementi firm is compared alongside a Broadwood grand dated 1801, there is no noticeable difference in the *quality* of workmanship, touch, or tone of the two models.[39] The only

William Frederick Collard (1776-1866).

[Portrait: John Collard's archive]

difference occurs in their tonal *character,* where the Clementi has a louder, more open, extrovert voice, whilst the Broadwood's tonal quality is more nasal, controlled, and less capable of changes in volume and tone colour. The interior design of the Clementi is not as sophisticated or as evolved as the Broadwood, however; and according to a contemporary witness in the year 1809, Clementi instruments were not so durable as Broadwoods, as a result of which they did not withstand changes in climatic conditions so well.[40]

William Collard, Frederick's younger brother, had a small investment in Clementi and Company by the year 1811. The surviving evidence suggests that William had skills in mechanical design and construction, whereas Frederick was perhaps more of a 'finisher' of completed instruments. William lived in Tottenham Court Road, where the keyboard instrument factory had been sited from the 1790s. Just like his older brother, William seems to have lived 'over the shop', or at least in a house adjoining the factory; his address was always given as Tottenham Court Road rather than Cheapside.

The siting of the Clementi factory in this particular part of London was a wise and deliberate choice: there was a considerable pool of expertise in the area – particularly in Soho, a few streets to the south, where German and Scottish piano makers had already been working for something like a forty-year period. John Geib, who had contracted to make square pianos for Longman and Broderip from the 1780s, also had a workshop in this part of London. After Geib closed down his business and emigrated to New York, it is likely that some of his skilled former employees would have been of value to the Clementi factory.

From the early 1800s, the Tottenham Court Road premises appears to have concentrated on the manufacture of square pianos, later extending the product range to include the earliest kind of upright piano, the so-called 'upright grand'. We have evidence to suggest that Clementi *grands* were being made at another address – for example, in a former harpsichord workshop within the City of London, where the last *harpsichord* makers became the earliest *grand* piano makers. When the small pencilled workmen's signatures which can be found in early Clementi instruments are analysed, we can detect an interesting overall pattern: many of the names found in the squares produced in Tottenham Court Road, such as *Zimmerman* (1805), *Neibuhr* (1810) and *J. Dettmer* (1829) are clearly those of German workmen. In contrast, those found in the grands, such as *Scott* (1807) *Robinson* (1812) and *Grey* (1815), are usually English surnames. This phenomenon, which needs further investigation, suggests that grand and square piano making, although both carried out in London, nevertheless represented two decidedly separate national traditions.

A huge tragedy befell the Clementi business in the year 1807: the Tottenham Court Road factory was burnt down to the ground in a disastrous fire. The entire stock of semi-manufactured pianos appears to have been lost, and production of instruments ceased abruptly. We know this latter fact for certain, because there is a very noticeable 'hold up' in the sequence of serial numbers for Clementi squares at this date. It is very noticeable, however, that there is no interruption to the sequence of serial numbers for grands at the same period – adding further circumstantial evidence to the probability of their being made elsewhere.[41]

William Collard's earliest patent is dated November 1811, and concerns his invention of a new kind of mechanical action for the 'upright grand'.[42] Before this date, the action mechanism for such pianos was quite cumbersome: the action and hammer mechanism actually lay *behind* the strings, and the hammers moved *towards* the player when they struck the strings. In order to remove such an action for repair, the tuner had to haul the piano into the middle of the room, remove a hinged panel from the back of the instrument, and then withdraw both the action and keys in the manner of a grand, but from the rear of the piano. In Collard's patent, the action is placed in front of the strings, between the player and the strings, and functions in the manner of a modern upright action. The patent specification also lists a feature directly derived from the grand: the *back check;* but this was certainly not the first time that back checks had been used in upright grands: those made in London by the Stodarts from the 1790s have back checks as a standard feature.[43]

By far the most important patent of William Collards is dated the 8th March 1821. With this patent, he introduced his amazing *Bridge of*

Reverberation and Harmonic Swell, a feature which was the forerunner of Steinway's 'Duplex Scaling' introduced fifty years later. Collard's system works in more or less the same way as Steinway's later one: in other words, the backlength of unwanted, unstruck string, instead of being permanently muted by a strip of listing cloth, is allowed to resonate in sympathy with the speaking length of the same string. In Collard's system, however, this interesting phenomenon only happens when a third foot pedal is depressed. The pedal mechanism is linked to a long damper arm which lies across the whole of the string backlengths in the piano. The raising of this long damper by the pedal frees the backlengths, and allows them to resonate sympathetically as the instrument is being played.

Collard's patent was applied to both the grand and the square piano.[44] In Steinway's 'Duplex' system, the sympathetic segments of string are much shorter than Collard's, and their lengths are meticulously calculated so that they may be tuned as accurately as possible in relation to the frequency of the struck part of the same string. In Collard's more primitive design, the back lengths are some three or four times the length of Steinway's, they are of random length, and they remain un-tuned.

When the necessary pedal of a Clementi instrument with a 'Bridge of Reverberation' is pressed down, and the long damper arm lifted away, the whole tonal character of the instrument is suddenly transformed: to the listener, it sounds as if the piano has inexplicably entered a huge cavern, with the sound of strings and hammers bouncing off its hard, rock walls. Others describe the effect as being as if the pianist was playing halfway up a steep alpine mountain, with the sounds echoing across the valleys, like an alphorn. Certainly, slow Swiss mountain melodies work well when performed with the 'Bridge of Reverberation'.

There seems little doubt that Collard's pioneering idea of 1821 had the support and blessing of Clementi himself, although, curiously, there does not appear to be any evidence in Clementi's published piano works suggesting the use of this device. On reflection, it has to be admitted that the whole idea was more of a clever sales gimmick, rather than being of profound musical benefit. It comes as no surprise when we discover that the 'Reverberation' idea was dropped after a few years: pianos made by the firm during the 1830s are of conventional internal design. Nevertheless, Collard's patent is certainly a milestone in the history of the piano, paving the way for Steinway's more evolved version of the same idea many years later.

After some thirty years as head of the firm, Muzio Clementi retired. At the age of seventy-nine and shortly before his death, he sold his interest in Clementi and Company to the two Collard brothers (1831). For many years after this date, the firm's pianos bore a black and gold name plaque with the cumbersome inscription: *Collard and Collard late Clementi and Company.*

Frederick Collard, the senior founding partner, died early in the year 1860, and a highly-interesting obituary appeared in the *Illustrated London News* of the 11th February of that year. The obituary is certainly worth quoting here:

> *The late Mr Collard. This celebrated pianoforte manufacturer, whose instruments are to be found in all parts of the world, and who has just died full of years and possessed of great wealth, was born at Wiveliscombe in Somersetshire in the year 1772. He came thence to London at the age of seventeen, with a few shillings in his pocket, to the house of Muzio Clementi, the celebrated theorist, player and pianoforte manufacturer in Cheapside. By great attention to the business, he at length succeeded in being admitted a partner, and the firm then became Messrs Clementi, Hyde, Banger, Davis and Collard. From that time to the day of his decease (excepting his annual three months' visit to Margate, where he was well known for his charitable acts during the last half century) he has always resided at Cheapside, dispensing there to the last a charitable hospitality. Mr Collard married early in life a Miss Lukey and a more amiable wife it was not possible for a man to be blessed with. She died about four years back, at the age of eighty-two, after a wedded life of nearly sixty years. The late Mr Collard did not like publicity to be given to the kind acts he did. His purse was always open to the well-authenticated statement of distress, and there are many who can speak of his liberality with grateful hearts.*
>
> *He used to tell, however, numerous anecdotes of the way he had been 'done' by some of the loose fish in the musical profession, but then only to laugh at his own want of discernment of their characters. Mr Collard's family have been extraordinary for their longevity. His father died at ninety-six, Mr Collard was eighty-eight, and a brother and sister survive him, each exceeding eighty years. The firm of Collard and Collard will be carried on by his two nephews (brothers) Frederick and Charles Collard who have assisted their uncle, as sole proprietor of the business, during the last twenty years.*

As we learn from the above obituary, Frederick Collard was the sole proprietor of the business for a twenty-year period before his death in 1860.

The reason for this was his younger brother's retirement from the partnership in 1842. William began a more leisurely existence at Folkestone, where he sat in the sun on the sea front enjoying a further twenty-four years of retirement until his eventual death on the 11th October 1866. William's inventiveness, which had been useful to the company, was continued by a certain James Stewart, Collard's technical director and factory manager. Stewart, a Scotsman, had emigrated to America as a young man in 1812, and had worked for a time in partnership with the eminent Boston piano manufacturer, Jonas Chickering. On his return to England sometime in the mid-1820s, Stewart was appointed factory manager of Clementi and Company, and shortly afterwards introduced an important innovation in piano construction which he patented on the 22nd March 1827.

This innovation is almost childishly simple, and yet it has become the basis of all modern piano stringing systems: his patent introduced the 'return string' into Collard pianos.[45] Before the year 1827, pianos had each of their strings (whether one, two or three for each note) individually terminating in a twisted 'eye', a tradition that harked back to the stringing of harpsichords and clavichords in the eighteenth century. It seems as if it had not occurred to any maker to turn a strand of wire back on itself to usefully form the second of a pair of identical strings to create a 'unison'. (However, in the museum at Cité de la Musique, Paris, there is a grand piano by the Parisian maker, Pascal-Joseph Taskin, dated 1788, which does indeed have a 'return' bicord system of stringing for all of its notes; and so Stewart's idea was not entirely new in 1827).

Stewart's idea, protected by patent, was clearly a time-saving device for the stringer more than anything else, although the 'return loops' were of benefit in helping to maintain a uniform 'downbearing' on the soundboard bridge. The idea also saves wastage in piano wire, which was an expensive item in 1827. There are no fewer than nine patents registered in the name of James Stewart between the years 1827 and 1859, and we assume that the Collard company was the beneficiary of all of them. Stewart must have also overseen the enormous rise in the number of pianos Collards made, as well as supervising the removal to a new factory in the year 1851. In the decade between 1820 and 1830, Clementi and Company was managing to make around 800 pianos each year. By 1840, the Collards had doubled this output to 1,600, a production figure which was maintained throughout the 1850s. From the early 1860s, output rapidly increased, so that by the year 1870 the number of instruments turned out by the firm had reached an impressive total of approximately 2,500 that year, or about fifty per working week.[46]

The increase in output in response to global demand for more and more pianos was made possible through the construction of an entirely new factory at Oval Road, near Regent's Park, in the year 1851. The new factory replaced the earlier Tottenham Court Road premises, and was designed and built in a most eye-catching manner: the factory was of circular construction, with windows placed around the full circumference of the building so as to enable the maximum amount of daylight to enter the premises. Such a design might have been inspired by the new, impressive railway engine turntable buildings which had become a prominent feature of the north London landscape by the mid century (one of which is now converted into the huge concert forum, *The Round House*).

Within a year of its completion, the new factory building tragically burnt down to the ground in an appalling fire (21st December 1851), of similarly disastrous proportions to Clementi's factory fire in Tottenham Court Road over forty years earlier. Although the building appears to have been insured, it was the loss of the workmen's tools by fire which was the greatest calamity; their possessions were certainly not insured. The fire began in an upper floor, and volunteers who lived nearby were able to rescue a number of the partially-finished instruments by entering the ground floor and quickly removing them out of the building. The fire soon ran out of control, however, largely as a result of the spreading of flames down an open lift shaft in the centre of the factory. When the roof finally fell in, it was realised that the whole building was lost. The sight of the immense conflagration was seen over many parts of north London that night.

Two days after the fire, a meeting of the workmen was held at the Stanhope Hotel, Camden Town. At the gathering, James Stewart proposed that a subscription list should be established in order to raise funds to pay for the lost tools. Soon, a list of over seventy firms and individuals promising funds was printed. Among the donors, the most generous was the Birmingham firm of piano wire drawers, Webster and Son, who pledged £25. William Collard sent ten guineas from Folkestone; the Camden Town firm of action makers Henry Brooks provided five guineas; James Stewart also provided five guineas; but the greatest surprise of all was the gesture on the part of piano makers John Broadwood and Sons, Collard's arch-rival: Broadwood workers actually raised ten guineas for Collard's benefit (in present-day terms, ten guineas is at least £1,000).

There were two outcomes of the 1851 fire: first of all, there was an unprecedented event: a grand 'evening concert' to raise money for piano

**The great Piano Factory Fire, 21st December 1851, as seen in the
Illustrated London News.**
[Illustration from Camden Local Studies Library, Holborn, London]

makers' tools was held at the Queen's Concert Rooms, Hanover Square, on the
16th January 1852. Among the pieces played on this occasion was Sterndale
Bennett's concerto for *three* pianos, just to remind the listening public that the
event was truly a piano one;[47] and of course the second outcome of the fire
was the immediate rebuilding of the Collard factory, on exactly the same site
as the destroyed edifice, and in exactly the same style and form as the first.
A second round factory was raised from the ashes in 1852, built by the firm of
Thomas and William Piper. It is this same building which survives in Oval

Road to this day. Now called *The Old Piano Factory*, the building was renovated in 1991 and converted into offices. It is in fact listed as a building of historical and architectural interest, and is well worth a visit to see.

The second round factory, the present building, was made as fireproof as possible by the construction of vaulted brick ceilings between all floors, although the hazardous lift shaft was still placed centrally, as in the earlier building. Piano production was arranged as follows: the back making and bellying (soundboard making) took place on the ground floor of the round factory; iron frames were fettled, finished and bronzed in a shed on the opposite side of Oval Road; the completed backs with their iron frames attached were then trundled off to yet another outbuilding, in which the noisy stringing process was carried out. The completed *upright* strung backs were next returned to the round building, and hoisted up to the top (fourth) floor, where the initial fitting up of casework for upright models was carried out. Assembly of uprights continued on the third floor, where parts such as doors, lids, legs, falls and columns were made and fitted. Underneath, on the second floor, upright action finishing, regulating and initial tuning took place; and then finally the uprights were lowered to the first floor, which was a warehouse and inspection room for checking the finished models before they were despatched.[48] By the mid 1920s, however, with contracting output, the top floor of the round building had apparently become a storeroom for parts and raw materials.[49] All stages of *grand* piano making – from rim bending to action finishing – were carried out in a separate, square building of four storeys height which immediately adjoined the round building of 1852. It seems likely that this additional square building had become a necessity once piano output began to expand during the 1860s and '70s.

The round building had two flaws, which were explained to the writer by the late Horace Singleton, who was apprenticed as a tuner in the Oval Road works during the early 1920s. According to Horace, by some oversight there were no factory windows which could be opened in this particular building; and so during the summer months, the employees were allowed to break the window glass in order to let in some ventilation. But in the winter, those same ventilation holes had to be boarded up with heavy wooden panels to keep out the unwelcome cold and draughts, and so daylight was somewhat restricted. A second flaw concerned the central hoist or lift: this was raised or lowered *manually* by some kind of cranking system tediously worked by a huge wooden lever. The top speed of this much-hated conveyor was *very slow*, and employees would waste a ridiculous amount of time just standing around waiting for the lift's arrival on their floor.[50]

Charles Lukey Collard (c. 1805-1891).
[Photo supplied by Richard Chapman]

It was this kind of inefficiency which certainly speeded up the eventual demise of the firm in 1929. It would have been no exaggeration to have described the Collard factory by the 1920s as 'Dickensian'; and yet in spite of the increasing out-datedness and continuing inefficiency of the firm's infrastructure, the workmanship and component quality of the Collard product remained very high, and this helped to retain loyal customers. There seems to have been a high level of loyalty from the hard-working workforce as well, who were very proud of their pianos.

For much of the second half of the nineteenth century, the day-to-day running of the firm was in the hands of Charles Lukey Collard (*c.* 1805-1891) who, as we noted earlier, was the nephew of the founding brothers. Charles was taken into partnership in the year 1831, when the business was purchased from old Clementi. From 1860, after the death of his uncle Frederick, Charles became sole proprietor of the firm, and soon became known as something of a 'tyrant'. His strong and forceful personality dominated his family as well as his employees. Something of his personality may be detected in the accompanying photograph, taken when he was an old man. In spite of possessing great wealth, Charles remained throughout most of his life a 'practical piano man'. He was particularly noted as being a good pianist with a 'particularly refined touch'.[51] He could also tune, regulate actions, and was a skilful hammer voicer.

There is one very interesting and curious story about Charles Lukey Collard: during the summer months, when he wished to spend time away from the factory and from London, he travelled to Somerset, where he had built in his native village of Wiveliscombe, at enormous cost, a huge mansion, complete with its own ballroom, named *Abbotsfields* (1870). The house still exists. Although he was far removed from the piano workplace, Charles nevertheless insisted that the firm's best grands should be sent down to him for the final inspection. Accordingly, a trainload of grands, along with a gaggle of skilled workmen, would leave Paddington Station, to make the long and tiresome journey to the West County. The grands would be taken off the train, delivered by horse and cart to Abbotsfields, and then placed in a long row in the ballroom. Whilst stationed at Wiveliscombe, the London employees would enjoy the pleasures of rural life and the hospitality of the house. Charles, often working alone, and sometimes by candlelight, would meticulously check over the quality of the instruments, making the final alterations and adjustments as necessary. Afterwards, the grands would be loaded-up in horse-drawn carts again, and taken to the local railway station. Those instruments not sold in the west country would have been transported back to London.

In this way, Collard was leading a double life – as a piano maker and as a country gentleman at the one and the same time. This kind of procedure appears to us today to be ridiculously inefficient, costly and time wasting. We tend to laugh at Charles Lukey Collard's seemingly unreasonable insistence that his firm's pianos should be sent all the way from London to his rural retreat in the west country, simply for checking. And yet, on reflection, the manufacture of grands in Japan or China today, and their costly and extravagant movement by ship halfway around the world for sale in Europe is, by the same standards, equally preposterous!

In the course of time, Charles was joined in business by two of his four sons: John Clementi Collard and Cecil Collard. The younger of the two, Cecil, was put in charge of the Oval Road factory. Between 1881 and 1885, Cecil introduced four patents, which are interesting in themselves, but not of any great significance in the evolution of the piano. Two of the patents are for small improvements to the 'sticker' upright action; a third patent (1885) features the interesting curiosity of a metal plate with studs on the piano's mainbridge, over which the strings pass, in place of the usual guide pins and carved notching; whilst a fourth patent (1881) introduced the long felt 'celeste' muting strip, worked by an extra pedal, into the *grand* piano. Such a feature is of course commonplace in Victorian over-damper, straight strung uprights, where the felt is placed vertically between hammer heads and strings; but in England, it had apparently never been seen in a grand before. The musical effect of the celeste pedal can be charming and delightful; but what Cecil Collard may not have realised is that exactly the same celeste or 'moderator' device is found as a standard feature in all grand pianos made in Vienna from the late eighteenth century.[52]

The grand finishing shop, Collard's factory, circa 1900. [Photo: Richard and Katrina Burnett's collection]

Immediately after the death of his father Charles in 1891, Cecil resigned as factory manager. This fact suggests that Cecil might have been pushed by his father into a career in which he had little genuine interest. Nevertheless, Cecil remained a 'sleeping partner' of the firm for the extraordinary span of a further thirty-eight years until his eventual death in 1929. It may be of significance that the demise of the Collard and Collard enterprise also happened in this same year, 1929, and so perhaps it was Cecil's long-term capital investment held within the family business which had enabled the firm to struggle on through the difficult trading times of the 1920s.

It was Cecil's older brother, John Clementi Collard (1844-1918) who was much more enthusiastic about running the long-established family business. He is remembered as being a charming, well-educated 'English gentleman', with many useful connections in the world of music and culture. He was not exactly a 'piano maker' – it is doubtful whether he had a great deal of practical knowledge of manufacturing – but he single-handedly undertook the running of the business for twenty-seven years from 1891, his particular skill being in the sales department.

In fact, John Collard was a great ambassador for the British piano, and made a number of exhausting sea voyages to such far-flung places as Australia and New Zealand, all in order to build up an impressive global clientele of dealers and distributors. In this respect, his activities were very similar to those of Horace Brinsmead, of John Brinsmead and Sons (see Chapter 1). Collard claimed to have sailed around the world on three successive occasions in his endeavours to promote his firm's pianos. During the earlier part of his career, the activity of piano making was highly remunerative, and 'Mr John' became an extremely wealthy man – in present-day terms, he was a multi-millionaire. As a result of his international sales activities, the firm's output of at least forty pianos each week was maintained up to the year 1900.

The latter part of his career, when he was in his seventies and still working, was fraught with the trauma of the First World War, the loss of orders, the acute shortage of essential raw materials, and of course the tragic loss of life of a significant proportion of the workforce as a result of warfare. By the year 1918, Collard and Collard output had declined to around twenty-three pianos per week; and later, throughout the 1920s, weekly output was rarely more than twelve pianos: two per day.[53]

John Collard's will, dated 1917, makes interesting reading.[54] Regrettably, perhaps, Mr John made no bequests of any kind to his loyal and hard-

The warehouse and showroom, Collard's factory, circa 1900. [Photo: Richard and Katrina Burnett's collection]

working employees in Oval Road, whose toil and sweat had created his wealth, other than one bequest of £50 to Charles Dewar, a senior employee. However, £300 (today, perhaps the equivalent of around £30,000) was conveyed under the terms of the will in trust to the Worshipful Company of Musicians in order to establish the charitable *Collard Fellowship*. The interest raised from the investment of the capital sum was used to support the careers of a number of well-known composers, including Sir Edward Elgar (in 1931) and Ralph Vaughan Williams (1934). The Collard Fellowship is still in existence, and it is still administered by the Worshipful Company of Musicians.

When he looked back on his long career in pianos, John Clementi Collard must have remembered in particular two notable events which affected his company. The first happened in the year 1896: he was working in his office one day, there was knock on the door, and a frail but distinguished-looking elderly lady entered. She was Miss Georgina Marian Kirkman (1828-1898), the last of a long and illustrious line of harpsichord and piano makers. She slowly sat down and, over a cup of tea, began to explain the reason for her visit: her brother, Henry Kirkman, had died over twenty years earlier (1874) and she had valiantly continued to run the firm's piano factory at Hammersmith.[55] She now wished to close down the company, but at the same time she was anxious to prevent the Kirkman name from falling into the 'wrong hands' and being used on instruments of inferior workmanship. It was her wish that Collard and Collard should take over both the goodwill and the stock of her company. Their conversation was recorded for posterity, and went something like this:

JCC: *'And the terms?'*
GMK: *'That you take the business as it stands, at certified cost.'*
JCC: *'And the name and goodwill?'*
GMK: *'An understanding that you will not dispose of it, and that you will continue to regard it on the same traditions as your own'.*
JCC: *'Yes, I am willing to do that; but the price?'*
GMK: *'That IS the price.'*

In other words, the value of the Kirkman goodwill was handed over to John Collard at no cost, provided that he undertook to continue to make Kirkman instruments which were of the same standard and quality as Collard's own. From 1896, then, Collard and Collard began to make the Kirkman piano in addition to their own make; but production of Kirkman instruments was always extremely limited, with no more than about thirty examples being produced each year.

The second event which John Clementi Collard must have reflected upon was the arrival in London, around the year 1906, of the brilliant Swedish piano designer, Johan Theodor Wennberg, who became something of a legendary figure in the London piano trade. Wennberg hailed from the city of Gothenburg in southern Sweden, where he had established a large piano factory by the early 1890s. Unfortunately, he ran into serious financial difficulties, and in December 1899 his company was declared bankrupt.[56] Having lost his home, his factory, and his family farm on Hissing Island as a result of the bankruptcy proceedings, Wennberg fled Sweden with his wife, in search of a new life and work; and some time after his arrival in England he was fortunate to be offered the position of Collard's works manager at Oval Road, a position he appears to have held for at least the next twenty years.

Wennberg's overstrung designs are probably the best instruments ever to leave the Collard factory. His pianos are distinguishable by the initials 'TW' cast into each iron frame, followed by a model number, such as TW1, TW2, TW3 and so forth.

By the 1920s, the firm's extensive factory premises were significantly under-used, but still carried high overheads. The vast timber yard adjoining the factory, where many large stacks of timber were once seasoned for seven years, now began to look semi-derelict. As production shrank, there was a general feeling of decay all around. It might have been a good idea for the firm to have sold off the timber yard for housing development in order to raise much-needed capital; but this did not happen. There was a feeling of pessimism from the firm's owners, who saw that films, gramophones, radio and then cars were slowly but surely beginning to replace the piano as the main source of family entertainment.

Matters were not helped by the arrival, in 1918, of a new managing director, Charles Wharton Collard (known as 'Wharton'), nephew of the energetic and enterprising Mr John. In contrast to his uncle, Wharton was considered by his family to have 'studiously neglected the business'.[57] He was the fourth generation of the Collard dynasty to be involved in the old-established firm, but it was clear that he did not share the same enthusiasm for piano making that his forebears had had. Wharton was very reluctant to

Collard's Round Factory, Oval Road, Regent's Park, circa 1920. [Photo: Richard and Katrina Burnett's collection]

invest in new plant, new machinery, a new electrically-operated hoist, or even new glass for the broken factory windows. It seemed to the employees that Wharton was simply biding his time, waiting for the inevitable closure of the dwindling business.

One of the serious problems which faced Collards at this time was the fact that the firm insisted on making its own keyboards and actions 'in house'. This was not at all cost-effective for the relatively small output which the firm had by the 1920s. There can have been few economies of scale within the action-making plant. The firm's piano components, in spite of their high quality, must have been expensive to produce. For many weeks, Wharton's nephew, Harry Marcy Collard (1902-1978) who was then under manager at the factory, had been trying to persuade his uncle to give up action and key making in favour of buying in the much cheaper Herrburger Brooks actions which were being made at nearby Lyme Street in Camden Town. Brooks actions were very well designed, of good component quality, and because of a huge volume in output they were very reasonably priced.

Eventually, after much persuasion, Wharton agreed to have a look at some of the Brooks mechanisms, and so a young sales representative arrived at the factory with samples. Harry was hopeful that the adoption of Brooks actions would help to turn round the ailing finances of the firm. Wharton was certainly impressed with the quality and price of the actions he examined, and to the relief of Harry he agreed to order a batch to try out in some models. But then the young representative asked if he could see Collard's own action and key-making department. Wharton kindly agreed, and proudly escorted the young man to that part of his old factory in which these processes were being carried out. The antiquated steam-driven machinery, and the laborious handwork being carried out by elderly dames in shawls and bonnets, so shocked and amused Brooks' young man that he collapsed into fits of laughter! Wharton was outraged, but did not show it to the visitor. As soon as the young representative had left the premises, he slammed his fist on the old oak desk in the office and shouted angrily to his nephew: 'We shall NEVER have Brooks actions on these premises!'[58]

It the year 1929, Collard and Collard Ltd was obliged to cease trading as a result of growing financial difficulties. The closure certainly did not come as a shock, in view of the situation we have just outlined. The last of the original Collard models, made during the late 1920s, were all of high quality, with fine ivory keyboards, choice veneers, and sturdy strung backs which stayed in tune well. The name and goodwill of Collard and Collard was purchased by the Chappell Piano Company Ltd, an American-owned business which, in contrast to Collards, was well capitalised and certainly go-ahead. Production of Collard instruments was moved into Chappell's extensive factory in Ferdinand Street, Chalk Farm, where some of the former Collard workforce must have gravitated.

Wharton immediately retired and lived on until 1944, spending time with a ladyfriend he had ensconced in a motor launch on the River Thames; but his nephew Harry joined Chappells for ten or so years, where he was responsible for sales of new Collard models. One of the curiosities of the Collard dynasty is that the family's piano trade connections were usually maintained by a *nephew* of a preceding generation, and Harry was no exception to this phenomenon. But in spite of having a fifth-generation Collard on the premises, the new instruments produced in Ferdinand Street were simply not Collards any more: they were Chappell designs with the Collard name attached (much in the same way that the Brinsmead name was attached to Cramer pianos after 1921). Great lengths were taken to disguise this fact from the piano-buying public, mainly because the loyal Collard dealer did not wish it to be known that the piano he was now selling was exactly the same instrument that the rival Chappell dealer was selling down the road in the same town.

And so Chappell iron frames were modified to have special 'Collard' features, and were finished in a different shade of bronze. Small modifications were also made to the casework of Collard models, to make them appear slightly different from the Chappells: a different style of column for an upright, for example, or a different design of music rest on a grand. From a musical and technical point of view, however, the Chappell and the Collard piano were identical instruments for the next forty years.

By the late 1960s, the Chappell factory had begun to assume some of the characteristics which Collard's Oval Road factory had in the 1920s: production was stagnating (grand piano making had almost stopped completely by 1965, and was dependent on a very elderly action finisher, Ralph Ralphs, who dutifully travelled in from retirement in Brighton a couple of days each week, just to keep grand production ticking over). During the 1950s and '60s, the workforce in Ferdinand Street never managed to construct more than one or two Collard instruments each week – usually the model 3 upright, and occasionally the small 4' 4" (132cm) baby grand.[59]

In 1970, the production of Chappell pianos was taken over by Kemble and Company Ltd of Milton Keynes, after which Kembles occasionally made a Collard model – but only if particularly pressed to do so by a dealer, which was never very often. The most we can say about the Collard and Collard piano today is this: the once famous brand name is, sadly, more or less in mothballs.

4

W. DANEMANN & COMPANY

W. DANEMANN and Company, which from time to time made some of the finest British pianos, was located throughout its long history in Islington, north London. The firm is best remembered for its robust school upright models, complete with almost indestructible heavy oak casework. These educational pianos, the '129' and the smaller model 'PJA', were highly regarded for their hard-wearing qualities, and they were the choice of many U.K. education authorities throughout the 1950s, '60s and '70s. These instruments were built down to a price, however, and did not represent the best of the firm's output. Danemann's best upright model, the HS2, was an outstanding instrument, but it achieved little fame as it was made in very limited numbers – perhaps never more than about twenty examples each year.

There has often been speculation as to the correct pronunciation of the firm's name. It is not *Daniman* but *Dane Man,* with the emphasis on the Danish sound.

Going back to the early 1890s, a young German architect and interior designer of the name William Danemann, who was born in the town of Wittenburg in or around the year 1864, had settled in London and had taken British citizenship. We do not know why he came to England, but it may be of significance that a certain August Danemann, another German, was in business as a furniture maker in Alderney Street, Pimlico, in the closing decades of the nineteenth century. It seems likely that the two Danemanns were related, although the precise connection has yet to be established.

William Danemann's work as a furniture designer, involving meticulous draftsmanship, was becoming well known. One day, according to family tradition, he received a commission from a small firm of piano manufacturers to design a series of piano cases. He spent many hours on the project, provided numerous drawings and sketches of casework options, and then sent in his account. To his astonishment, the firm in question had gone into receivership, and Danemann was never paid. So what did he do? He went round to the liquidators, discussed matters, and then offered to buy the piano-making business – with a reduction in the purchase price in consideration for what he was owed for the design work. And so William Danemann, on impulse, became a piano manufacturer. He knew nothing about the technology of piano construction, but his skilful eye for furniture design must have helped to achieve sales in those early days.[60]

William Danemann commenced business at Islington in the year 1893, in Northampton Street, where the firm was to remain throughout its existence. For the next fifty-five years, the company built 'trade' pianos; in other words, anonymous instruments sold to music shops, which usually had dealers' names or trademarks on the fallboards above their keys. In this respect, Danemann was one of a large group of 'trade makers' in London during the first half of the twentieth century, a group which also included the firms of Brasted, Bansall, Cremona, Kemble, Triumph, Spencer, Squire and Zender. This explains why it is quite unusual to find any piano bearing the name 'Danemann' before the year 1950. After the Second World War, however, there was a deliberate change in the firm's marketing policy: it would no longer make trade instruments, but only pianos bearing the founder's surname.

By the 1920s, William Danemann had been joined in business by three of his sons, Frederick, Edgar and Edward. Of these three, Frederick (born *circa* 1896) was tragically killed in 1934, when a tree fell on a car in which he was driving. He was the father of the famous stage and TV actor, Paul Daneman (who spelt his surname with only one 'n'), and grandfather of the well-known professional singer, Sophie Daneman. William's second son, Edgar Ludwig (1898-1977) became involved in the technicalities of piano construction, and as well as being the firm's scale designer for many years, he also took on the responsibility of 'passing out' each new piano as it left the Northampton Street factory.

The Danemann piano works, Northampton Street, Islington, 1930s.
The factory was extended to the left of the goods entrance at a later date.
[Photo: Jacqui Winchester's archive]

Edgar used to tell of the time, shortly before the First World War, when he was gaining experience in a factory in Russia which apparently belonged to a distant relation. One of his work pals was Russian, another German. Shortly before the outbreak of hostilities, Edgar hurriedly left Russia and only just managed to make it to the frontier before it closed and hostilities commenced. His Russian colleague joined the Russian army, while his German friend enlisted in the German military. Edgar himself saw active service in the British army in the First War, and was partially blinded by shrapnel as a result. After the war, however, he had a surgical operation, which greatly improved his eyesight.

The youngest of the three brothers, Edward Richard (born 1904) was known as 'Tom'. His role within the firm was to take charge of sales and the ordering of piano parts from suppliers. Tom Danemann had the misfortune of being a polio victim, and had lost the use of one leg. Instead of using the normal calliper and built-up shoe, Tom preferred to use a wooden crutch. One of these crutches, in solid oak, satin finish, he used when he had to stomp around the factory in overalls, trouble shooting. This crutch was put to

Relaxing at a Trade Fair in the 1950s: from left to right:
Tom Danemann, Jo Seabridge (company secretary) and Edgar Danemann.
[Photo: Jacqui Winchester's archive]

remarkable use in 1972, when Tom was able to foil a 'wages snatch' near the factory, beating off his attackers by using his oak crutch as a club. Another crutch, in ebony high polish, was reserved for special occasions, when dark-suited Danemann attended important business functions, such as a Trade Fair.

In the year 1934, an event occurred which was to have great benefit for the Danemann company: the West Yorkshire piano manufacturer, Pohlmann and Son of Halifax, decided to close down its factory. An agreement was reached whereby W. Danemann and Company, as a 'trade maker', would henceforth manufacture Pohlmann instruments in London, under licence, and the Halifax firm would receive a royalty of £2 for each piano sold. Many of the new pianos made under this agreement would have been sold in Pohlmann's retail shop in Halifax. The agreement between Henry, Frederick and Arnold Pohlmann and William, Edgar and Tom Danemann is dated the 7th June 1934. Under its terms, all the various designs, patterns, jigs, templates and so forth to make the Pohlmann instruments were removed from Halifax and placed in the Islington factory.[61]

At this point, we must digress a little and mention something about Henry Pohlmann (1893-1978), a director of the Halifax firm and party to the 1934 agreement. As a young man, Henry had been sent by his father to study piano design at the German factory of the famous Grotrian Steinweg company, situated at Brunswick. On his eventual return to Halifax, Henry evolved an excellent upright scale design, no doubt inspired by his time in the Grotrian works; and from 1934, this same 'scale' became available for Edgar Danemann's use as a basis for his own design work. The so-called 'Pohlmann scale' was the foundation of Danemann's best upright, the HS2. In fact, the Pohlmann scale was so revered and cherished that it was not only used in other upright models, but also incorporated into the scale design of some of the interesting range of grands which Danemann introduced some years later, in the 1950s. The details of the 'Pohlmann scale' are shown in Appendix 5.

A very unusual feature which Edgar Danemann introduced into his firm's uprights and grands during the 1930s is the so-called 'back bridge': a counter bridge of beech, which is glued to the back of the soundboard, and with cutouts to allow the soundboard ribs to pass under it. The back bridge follows exactly the lines and contours of the pinned bridge (over which the strings pass on the other side of the soundboard). As far as the author is aware, this feature had never before been used by any British manufacturer, although it had long been a constructional feature of the German Ritmuller piano, and may even be found in Pleyel grand pianos made in Paris during the second quarter of the nineteenth century. So Edgar Danemann was not the originator of the idea. Its use in Danemann pianos, however, does much to give his firm's instruments their distinctive tonal colour, with a highly-pleasing, long sustaining power.

There are other benefits from using the 'back bridge': first of all, the soundboard is made stronger and more rigid as a result, and, in theory, is better able to withstand the downbearing pressure from the stringing load. Secondly, the presence of the back bridge helps to eliminate what is often a noticeable tonal weakness in those strings lying next to the point where the cast-iron frame bar passes through a trough in the wooden pinned bridge. Thirdly, the back bridge helps a 'smoother' and more even tone quality from register to register; and fourthly, a back bridge functions as something of a clamping device, helping to keep the soundboard ribs in place. This function was of particular advantage in instruments sold to customers in tropical climates, where there was always the risk of high humidity weakening the glue joints between ribs and soundboard. In spite of the structural and acoustic benefits of the back bridge, the added rigidity as a result of its presence reduces the dynamic range of the instrument; and probably for this reason, its use has never gained general popularity among piano makers.

*The highly-skilled 'bellyman', Albert Martin, using a go-bar press to
glue the rim and back bridge to an upright piano soundboard, Northampton Street works,
Islington, early 1970s.*

[Photo: Author's collection]

As we noted earlier in this chapter, after the Second World War, the Danemann firm underwent a transformation: it ceased to make trade pianos altogether (even Pohlmanns) and within a few years had introduced a range of large, high-quality grands. The firm had made a quite deliberate and dramatic move 'up market', and in 1951 had the honour of providing a newly-designed concert grand for the recently-built Royal Festival Hall, on London's south bank. The way in which the Danemann company had evolved over a few years was certainly impressive, and the company was obviously proud of its new achievements in the realm of piano construction.

The driving force behind these important developments was the young Peter Danemann (1926-1987), who represented the third generation of the family attached to the business. He was Edgar's son. Like his father, Peter had a deep interest in piano construction: it was a fascinating subject for him. There are stories told of family gatherings at Sunday lunchtimes, when Edgar, Tom and Peter and their wives would sit down to a hearty meal. Throughout the gathering, there was really only one topic of conversation from the men: pianos. This of course quickly became annoying for all the females present! Peter had studied scale design under Sydney Hurren at the Northern Polytechnic, Holloway Road, where he had learnt such important skills as string tension calculation, scale layout planning, correct hammer strike points, and technical drawing. On completion of his training, he worked on the shop floor of the family factory, gaining practical experience. Then he designed and produced his first two upright models, a small upright called 'PJ' and an even smaller model named 'PJA'. These designs became the basis of all the successful small domestic uprights offered by the firm between the 1950s and the 1980s.

Next, Peter Danemann turned his skills to grand piano design. Before the Second War, the firm produced only small grands, in particular a baby model of only 4' 3" (129.5cm) length. These grands were part of a fleet of 'trade' models, in which price and compact furniture design were the most important features, and the inferior bass tone associated with such short instruments was of less concern to the purchaser. Two large grand models materialised from Peter Danemann's drawing board during the early 1950s: the model PJB, a boudoir instrument of length 6' 8" (203cm), and then a full-sized concert grand, the model PJC, of length nine feet (275cm). At the same time, Edgar was working on the design of a 5' 2" baby grand (157cm) to replace the smaller and somewhat musically-inferior baby grands of pre-war date.

The well-loved 'Pohlmann scale' was utilised in Peter's two large grands, but not in Edgar's smaller design. In the case of the concert instrument, the

Pohlmann scale was used initially for the string lengths from the top note (c88) down to c40 (middle c). However, the Danemanns were clearly not satisfied with the top treble sound of this particular model. Modifications were made, as we discover from notes made by Peter on the 27th October 1978:

> *Feurich. This grand which ELD and I came across had a remarkable treble (c88 to c52 say). It was so impressive we took all the measurements (rubbing of the scale, etc. now lost) and drew it out and used it on the concert grand'.*[62]

The new Danemann grands of the early 1950s were admired and sought after, and they were reasonably priced. An important customer was the former London County Council, who over the years ordered no fewer than fourteen concert grands and twenty-two boudoir grands for use in school halls and public buildings. By the 1960s, the firm had provided over two hundred boudoir models for use in various educational establishments in and around London. Danemann also gained a lucrative government contract to supply grands to British embassies: forty-six boudoir models were shipped

Danemanns on display – location unrecorded – early 1950s.
[Photo: John Broadwood and Sons Ltd]

Sid Smith stringing a Danemann 6' 8" grand. Northampton Street, Islington, early 1970s.

[Photo: Author's collection]

from Northampton Street to embassies in all parts of the world during the 1950s and '60s. It is probably accurate to state that Danemann, with Challen, had the largest grand output of any London manufacturer at this period.

Of course, the feather in the firm's cap was the concert grand ordered for the Royal Festival Hall in 1951. This was followed up by an order for the same-sized model from the new Sibelius Concert Hall at Helsinki in Finland. It is sad to relate, however, that the Danemann company was slow to build on its immediate post-war success in the field of concert instruments. There appeared to be a minimal 'after sales' service of the kind which the Challen company had been able to provide for its BBC grands. The Danemann directors, with their long history of making cheaper 'trade pianos' at the 'sharp end' of the market, found it hard to adapt to the tricky and stressful job of servicing concert instruments to a high standard, and by the early 1970s, the company had more-or-less given up its dalliance with the difficult world of concert pianos. There was insufficient contact with concert pianists, in order to pander to their requirements. The somewhat Puritan and even Philistine world of the Northampton Street factory could be less than sympathetic to the world of the performing concert artist. Steinway and Sons' sophisticated and better-funded after-sales service had won them a near monopoly in the main London concert halls by the 1970s.

Peter Danemann's day-to-day role within the factory was that of 'middle management'. He was involved in progress chasing, technical trouble-shooting, and quality control, all of them stressful jobs. Although he became a director and shareholder of the company, he remained very much under the control of his father and uncle. This inevitably led to family disputes. One morning, following a heated row at the factory, Peter simply put on his coat and walked out, sadly never to be seen again by the workforce, who had always admired his design expertise.

He seemed to have left the piano trade for good, and established with his wife a successful elderly persons' home in Bedfordshire. So it came as a great surprise when Peter returned to piano making many years later, in 1980; he opened a small workshop at Woburn Sands, Bedfordshire, and, trading as *Peter Danemann Pianos,* began to assemble an elegant-looking prototype baby grand. His long-held fascination with pianos was obviously far too difficult for him to overcome! Sadly, his death at the early age of sixty-one in 1987 prevented his hope of developing manufacture at Woburn Sands from coming into fruition.

A small Danemann 'spinet' upright, based on the 'PJA' strung back, circa 1960.
[Illustration from a Danemann publicity brochure]

Back at the old family factory at Northampton Street, Islington, Edgar and Tom Danemann had been focussing the firm's activities from the 1960s on the building of school upright pianos in considerable quantities, rather than developing grand manufacture; and of course the Danemann company is best known for its upright educational instruments. At one point during the early 1970s, the manufacture of school uprights comprised about 80% of the firm's total annual output. We sometimes wonder if the Danemanns saw themselves as 'piano makers to the State', in view of the fact that their biggest customers by far were local education authorities.

Danemann school models are renowned for their toughness and durability, but many of them tend to have a 'clangy' and aggressive tonal quality, which might be good to fill a classroom with sound, but not so pleasing to the ear. There is a simple explanation for this phenomenon: Edgar Danemann insisted on having 'hard' felt hammers inside his school pianos.

He repeatedly asked his hammer suppliers, Herrburger Brooks, to make them *really hard*. Perhaps he felt that a noisy and stinging hammer blow would help to overcome the deadening acoustic qualities which heavy oak casework usually has. Danemann domestic instruments, on the other hand, usually have a warmer and more gentle tonal quality as a result of the softer, heavier, and more expensive hammer felts used in these particular instruments.

The company received orders for its school instruments from leading educational buyers, such as Kent, Surrey and the West Riding County Councils, whose purchasing departments put in huge bulk orders for school models. Danemann was therefore obliged to offer very attractive discounts for the bulk orders, which meant that the firm ended up selling school pianos directly to educational authorities at wholesale prices, or even less. To the average piano retailer, this seemed very unfair, as they themselves were often undercut in price by the manufacturer when tendering for the supply of school instruments. In fact, this unpopular 'direct selling' from manufacturer to end user so offended the high street retailers that many of them refused to stock Danemann instruments altogether, and this in turn led to a significant dwindling in the numbers of domestic instruments made at Northampton Street. During a typical working week in the early 1970s, for example, perhaps no more than four or five domestic uprights left the factory.

Danemann retained a few valuable retail customers, however, such as Forsyths of Manchester and Harrods of Knightsbridge. The excellent HS2 upright was specially manufactured for Harrods. Externally, it looks identical to Danemann's standard 'Classic' domestic model; internally, however, the HS2 was described by the workforce as being 'out of this world' because of its high-quality, specially-selected components. During production stages at the factory, when the progress of any particular HS2 model was being chased up, the oft-heard question was: 'Where is that Out-of-this-World piano?' Its features included ivory-covered keys, Renner action and hammers from Stuttgart, and a soundboard made from the choicest and most costly Romanian pine available to the Trade – of violin maker's quality.

Only a few hundred HS2s were turned out of Northampton Street during the 1960s and '70s, and all of them were sold through Harrods. One of the fascinating things about this particular model is the way in which it demonstrates how a good choice of soundboard timber can profoundly affect tonal quality for the better. The HS2 stands head and shoulders tonally above the firm's standard 'Classic' model, fitted with a much cheaper coarser-grained sitka spruce soundboard, even though both the Classic and the HS2 share exactly the same design of iron frame and have identical 'Pohlmann' stringing scales.

The Danemann school uprights were built to very rigid specifications, laid down during the late 1940s and early 1950s. Such instruments were required to have solid oak case components, and expensive-to-produce wire gauze protective backing pieces behind their soundboards. Part of the same rigid specification, which was initiated by the former London County Council, insisted that the instruments had to be at least four feet in height (122cm) and that their internal timber construction had to be based on a massive six-post braced back. The specification even laid down the type of steel piano wire which must be employed: zinc plated, and therefore rust-resistant. This kind of music wire, which was specially drawn in Scotland, was certainly tonally inferior to the unplated, polished steel wire of German origin; but then those involved in the laying down of specifications were uneducated in this important area of piano-building knowledge.

The obligations outlined in the previous paragraph made the Danemann school instruments quite costly to produce. Large quantities of choice solid oak had to be kept in stock for months in order to season on the flat roof of the factory, and this tied up the firm's working capital. At the same time, the pianos had to be competitively priced in order for the firm to gain the bulk orders it desired. By the late 1960s, the company was making only about £5 profit on each piano produced. Then, during the 1970s, the rigid specifications for school models were relaxed: cheaper veneered oak parts (rather than solid oak) were now acceptable, and smaller instruments were actually preferred by the teaching profession, whose music-teaching members could now see over the top of their instruments. This helped them to direct classroom singing, and enabled them to better maintain classroom discipline. Other manufacturers, builders of budget instruments such as Zender and Bentley, offered smaller, cheaper educational pianos than Danemann's, but always without wooden braced backs, and with cheaper safety castors attached to simple, screw-on brackets.

It certainly became increasingly difficult, as the 1970s progressed, for the Danemann firm to make a good living from the production of decent-quality educational models. The morale of the company was kept up, however, by the arrival of an occasional 'prestige' order, such as requests for large batches of instruments destined for the rehearsal rooms of the Royal College of Music, Kensington, or the Royal Northern College of Music, Manchester.

Danemann school upright piano in heavy, functional, oak casework, circa 1975.
[Photo: Author's collection]

The continuity of production at Northampton Street was very much helped by the existence of a loyal, highly-skilled workforce, some of whom gave years of service to the company. We can mention in particular Charlie Samuels, the back shop foreman, who had spent over fifty years of his working life with Danemanns before his retirement in the early 1980s. His knowledge of the assembly of wooden braced backs, soundboards, bridges, iron frames and strings, accumulated as a result of a half-century's experience, was in all probability unequalled in the Trade, and so he was obviously a great asset to the company. He knew every trick, from the shrinking of soundboards before the ribs were attached, to rapid rib bonding using hot glue and a traditional 'go bar' press. Samuels was one of the world's 'natural gentlemen', and as a result, the atmosphere within the firm's backmaking shop (situated at the rear of the premises, in a well-lit single-storey shed with overhead windows) was usually pleasant, friendly, and well organised.

Fred Craven, Danemann's grand finisher, balancing a set of grand keys, early 1970s.
[Photo: Author's collection]

The firm also employed an exceptionally-skilled grand finisher, Fred Craven, who worked in the first-floor shop and had responsibility for regulating and checking over the half-dozen grands the firm made each month. There was also loyalty to be found in the administration: the company secretary, Josephine Seabridge, had given something like forty years' service before her retirement in 1977. We must not forget to mention the long-suffering upright action-finishing foreman, a certain Woodgate, who had a favourite expression as things started to go wrong when an apprentice made a serious mistake: 'You are a headache in my backside', he would miserably declare.

Edgar Danemann and his younger brother Tom had a very good business partnership, Tom being very much the 'tough businessman' who, more than his elder brother, shouldered the role of general manager of the firm and was better known in the Trade because of his travels as a salesman for the company. Edgar, on the other hand, was a rather shy, retiring figure, who chose to spend a considerable portion of his working day on the shop floor, dressed in drab overalls and supervising production. There was many a smartly-dressed sales representative, who on entering the factory, would mistake Edgar for one of the employees and demand to see the general manager. Edgar, as owner of the business and of the factory building itself, would peer over his glasses and modestly point the visitor in the direction of the general office.

Each day, Edgar could be found in the small 'looking over' room at the front of the factory, checking every upright piano before it left the works. He ran a factory of sixty employees with the aid of a small pencil tucked over one ear and a small notebook placed in the top pocket of his overalls. By the 1980s, he had been replaced by an office-full of computers – which helped to make the firm's administration top heavy, and speeded up the demise of the business. Those individuals within the office who sat for hour-upon-hour in front of their computers, dazzled by the glamours of the new computer technology, were certainly pressing the *wrong* keyboards. It might have been better for the firm if they had spent time carefully checking over the keys of their products, just as old Edgar Danemann had done a few years previously.

It was largely because of Edgar's diligence that the standard of action work in the firm's pianos was maintained at such a high standard during the 1960s and '70s. If you had walked into any retail piano shop during this period and carefully compared the standard of mechanical regulation found in the London-made pianos on display there, you would have found a wide range. Some of the regulation was rough, and a discredit to the industry. Sales of London-made pianos were significantly damaged during the 1970s and '80s, because their overall quality of action regulation was not on a par with that found in the Japanese Yamaha or Kawai, and any competent pianist or piano teacher could soon feel that the Japanese action movements were more responsive to the touch when compared with many of the British pianos in the same price category. The industry's excuse was a lame one: 'We simply can't find the skilled men any more,' its directors would bleat.

Edgar's maintenance of high standards was certainly helped by the conscientious work of his skilled action finishers – individuals like Tom Chubb, Ernest Chalkley (formerly of Chappells), Alan Futcher (formerly of Kembles) and Stan Job. This team helped to ensure that small but important details, such as an even touch depth, or the correct bedding angle for the back checks, or the precise placing of the damper shade rail so that it functions as it is meant to do, were properly attended to. They worked alongside two skilled tuner/voicers, Horace Singleton and Terry Peacock, and three blind tuners, Otto Reeves, Francis Nash and John Wharton.

Checking a PJA upright piano in the looking-over room at his Northampton Street factory: Edgar Danemann, early 1970s.
[Photo: Author's collection]

Edgar Danemann died on a cold winter's night in February 1977, aged 79. He had never retired. One morning, he simply didn't show up for work, and his death was announced shortly afterwards. At the time of his death, a fourth generation of the proprietors' family was involved in the business: Jacqui Danemann, Peter Danemann's eldest daughter, had arrived in 1975 and remained for a five-year period, taking over Josephine Seabridge's role as office manager. Jacqui was married, and the arrival of two small babies soon curtailed her piano trade activities. At one period in the mid 1970s, her younger brother Tim was also seen at the factory, working as an action finisher with Ernest Chalkley. Tim spent only six months in Northampton Street before deciding to leave, but he had not lost interest in pianos: he assisted his father in the setting up of the workshop at Woburn Sands during the 1980s, and helped him construct the prototype grand we have previously mentioned. Today, Tim Danemann is to be found at Buckfastleigh in Devon, where he runs a small business involved in tuning, repairing and restoring pianos.[63]

After 1980, the administration of the Danemann business fell upon the shoulders of Tom Danemann, by now in his late seventies. He must have become more and more tired, weary and stressed because his firm faced a worsening financial situation and was losing money. His closing months with the firm were saddened when the very last concert grand made by the company fell from its first-floor hoist at the factory as it was being loaded onto a lorry, and was destroyed. The piano was not insured.

It must have been a very welcome moment for Tom in 1982 when he shook hands with Adam Johnstone, chairman of John Broadwood and Sons Ltd, and agreed to sell the whole of the business and the factory premises to Broadwoods. Shortly afterwards, Tom retired, and new Broadwood pianos began to be made at Northampton Street. The Danemann workforce now had to adapt to new arrangements: they had to learn how to construct a range of at least six Broadwood grand and upright instruments in addition to the eight Danemann models already in regular production. There were far too many slightly-differing designs of piano being constructed at the factory during the early 1980s. Some rationalisation of product range was badly needed, but this did not happen.

Edgar Danemann's baby grand piano, early 1950s, clad in a 'contemporary' casework designed by Ward and Austin.

[Photo: John Broadwood and Sons Ltd]

The financial problems which had for some years clouded life for the Danemann firm refused to go away; and so the parent company, John Broadwood and Sons Ltd, in need of capital, decided to take out a loan of £250,000 with Islington Borough Council in order to 'help maintain jobs in the Borough of Islington'. Sadly, the loan repayments could not be met, and within a matter of months the Borough Council was forced to call in the Official Receiver – on the 2nd July 1984. Ninety years of piano manufacturing in Northampton Street lurched to a sudden halt. The firm of W. Danemann and Company Ltd was eventually wound up in the High Court of Justice on the 21st January 1985, although the parent company, Broadwood, managed to survive.

The summer of 1984 was certainly a sad moment for the British piano industry. Danemann's was the last of the once-numerous north London piano factories. The closure of the premises and the dismissal of the workforce destroyed a pool of piano-making expertise, the likes of which could never be re-assembled in this country. In its own way, the Danemann factory and its reservoir of skills had been something of a National Treasure. In a more enlightened age, it might have been saved. The empty factory was soon converted into office premises and renamed *The Ivories*. The architect who carried out the conversion set up a pair of smart iron gates in front of the former goods' entrance. The gates are shaped in the form of two interlocking grand pianos – a kind of commemorative gesture.

For many in the Trade, July 1984 seemed like the end of the road for Danemann; but it wasn't. To everyone's amazement, a family of Welshmen from Cardiff – a father and two sons – suddenly turned up at Northampton Street and made an offer, not only for the Danemann name, designs and goodwill, but also for a substantial part of the work in progress. The three individuals were Robert Gardner and his sons Stephen and Jeffrey. Their offer was accepted by the Receiver, and within a short period, lorry-loads of piano components were on their way to Cardiff. At a little later date, a few of the former key personnel from the Danemann factory, such as Albert Martin the highly-skilled soundboard maker, were also seen driving to Cardiff, to assist the Gardner family in the setting up of piano production at their Leckwith Place workshop.

The Gardners decided to concentrate on the manufacture of two upright models: the 'Classic', and the smaller 'PJA'. (Production of the range of Danemann grands could not be re-started because the master patterns for the grand frames had been wilfully destroyed by the ironfounder who had also gone out of business as a result of the Northampton Street liquidation.) Over the next ten years, Gardner's workshop managed to produce a few dozen PJA models (either in educational or domestic form); but the Welsh firm's most successful item by far was the well-known 'Classic' design, of which some 350 examples were finished in Cardiff. Throughout their time as piano makers,

From left to right: Jo Seabridge (company secretary), Tom Danemann, and
Charlie Samuels (back shop foreman), photographed circa *1972 shortly after Tom had*
foiled a wages snatch by using his crutch as a club.

[Photo: John Broadwood and Sons Ltd]

the Gardners were not satisfied to 'rest on the laurels' of the London Danemanns: they were constantly experimenting and modifying their piano designs as they saw fit, introducing new features such as 'floating' soundboards (in which the edges or fillets of the soundboards are freely suspended in the region of their bass bridges in order to improve the resonance in the bass register). They also re-calculated and modified both Pohlmann's and Peter Danemann's original string scalings.

The last Cardiff Danemann was produced in 1994. The firm decided to cease manufacturing because, in the words of Jeff Gardner, 'Slowly and surely the market began to dry up as the wave of imported pianos from the Far East forced prices down'. Today, the firm of Gardner Piano Specialists still owns the 'Danemann' registered trademark, and pianos bearing the name are now made in China for sale in the Cardiff shop. The treasured jigs and templates for the production of the original models of Danemann upright have not been destroyed, however: they are safely in store, waiting for that sunny day when (once again in the words of Jeff Gardner): 'Should conditions favour it, we will dip our toes into the water and restart piano production'.[64]

5
WELMAR

THE Welmar history falls into three parts, the first of which began in 1919, when a south London 'trade' manufacturer named *Cremona Ltd* of Medlar Street, Camberwell, was commissioned to produce new pianos to which the trademark *Welmar* was attached. The second part of the history commenced in 1934, when Whelpdale and Maxwell Ltd, who were the actual owners of the *Welmar* trademark, opened up their own new factory at Clapham, south London. Through negotiation with the liquidators of the now-defunct Cremona company, Whelpdales managed to acquire the earlier Cremona designs and the wherewithal to manufacture. These were successfully used at Clapham in order to maintain the manufacture of Welmar instruments for a further seventy years. The third phase of the history began in 2003, when, following the closure of the Welmar factory, new pianos bearing the brand name, and made in China, began to be imported by Intermusic Ltd, a firm with an office and warehouse at Poole in Dorset.

The Germanic sound of the name *Welmar* may have helped piano sales. During the 1920s and '30s, an imported piano from Germany could usually be depended upon to have good quality touch and tone. But the name 'Welmar' is certainly not German, nor were the firm's instruments ever of German origin or design. The brand name is simply an amalgamation of the two surnames 'Whelpdale' and 'Maxwell', founding partners of the London firm established in 1876 in order to import into Britain the famous *Blüthner* pianos, made at Leipzig in Germany. Whelpdale and Maxwell Ltd (known after 1945 as Whelpdale, Maxwell and Codd Ltd, after Jack Codd was taken into partnership) continued its Blüthner-importing activities throughout the twentieth century.

Was the choice of the name 'Welmar' a wise decision or not? It would have been very hard to have sold any piano, no matter how fine-toned, with the rambling name *Whelpdale, Maxwell and Codd* proudly displayed on its nameboard. Such a title is more appropriate for a practice of old-established country solicitors rather than for a make of piano. To many people, however, even those with only a smattering of German, the name Welmar seems a little bogus. We cannot but help wondering if, from 1919, Whelpdales were hoping that their customers might believe that they were actually purchasing a piano with Germanic associations. (The author once heard an individual praising in a refined Oxford accent the qualities of his 'Velmar' piano!)

Whatever the virtues or otherwise of the name, there are a number of things we know for sure about the British-made Welmar piano: it is usually very well designed internally and tastefully designed externally; it usually has very good tonal qualities – in fact there are only a few British makes which can equal the Welmar in this respect. Along with the Broadwoods and the Chappells, the Welmars were once the most expensive British pianos on the market; and the Clapham Park Road works had the satisfaction of turning out a steady stream of well-made, solid and dependable musical instruments for seventy years. At one period, the firm went as far as to claim in its advertising that its products were 'Britain's finest pianos'. This bold assertion never appears to have been disputed.

The new factory in Clapham Park Road might have been seen at first as something of a 'sideline' by Whelpdales, whose main business lay with the importation and selling of the expensive Blüthner instruments (particularly grands) in considerable quantities. As a result of the Second World War and its aftermath, however, Blüthner pianos were not available in Britain for a period of at least eleven years – from 1939 until the early 1950s – and so the London factory assumed much greater importance during this period, being the source of pianos which the firm could sell, either in its West End London showrooms or through regional piano shops.

As if to demonstrate that there was some kind of 'Blüthner continuity' from the late 1930s to the early 50s, the internal features of the London-built Welmar models were deliberately styled to look as Blüthner-like as possible. The cast-iron frames for the firm's grands, for example, were superficially modified to closely resemble the frames of Blüthner design. The same iron frames were bronzed in a shade particularly associated with the Leipzig maker; and even the listing and bearing cloth strips under the stringing were dyed in a special shade of royal blue, still known to the Trade as 'Blüthner blue'. The lightly-ribbed Welmar soundboards were noticeably modelled on the lightly-ribbed Blüthner ones; and the attached bass bridges were almost carbon copies of the very unusual type seen in the instruments from Leipzig.

The disclosure of this technical information is not done to imply that the Whelpdale company was in any way attempting to 'deceive' its customers. The adoption of Blüthner-like features in London was done out of sheer admiration for the Leipzig product; and for many years, a label was inserted into each instrument clarifying the situation, and stating that the Welmar piano was produced by Blüthner and Co in London, and was not to be confused with the famous Blüthner piano of Leipzig. However, it is clear that the Whelpdale firm was hoping that its own London-produced instruments would be seen as good substitutes at a time when supplies from Leipzig had dried up (1939-1950). This helps to explain how for many years, the Welmar instrument was popularly-known in the Trade as the 'English Blüthner'.

(We should emphasise here that the German company, which always had an excellent and friendly relationship with its British importers, nevertheless never allowed any of its own models and designs to be manufactured under licence at the Clapham Park Road factory. In retrospect, we can only suggest that it might have helped the longer-term survival of London production if the German company *had* kindly consented to such an arrangement!)

As we noted in the introduction to this chapter, the range of models which were long sold as 'Welmars' originated as the products of Cremona Ltd, of Medlar Street, Camberwell. The four individuals who played a role in the creation and then the evolution of the Cremona product were Clarence Lyon, Charles Squire, Edmund Whomes and Alfred Knight.

Clarence Edward Lyon (1883-1960) founded Cremona Ltd in 1914. He came from a long line of London piano makers: his father, Louis George Lyon (1865-1941) had a piano factory in Camberwell Road from the 1880s, where Clarence was trained; his grandfather Frederick Lyon was also in business as a piano maker. In fact, the surname Lyon, probably of Scottish origin, is traceable in London piano-making circles as far back as the year 1812.[65] Clarence Lyon chose the name *Cremona* for his newly-established firm because of his admiration for the tonal qualities of the violins made in the north Italian town of that name. Lyon was the firm's scale designer. He drafted out the layout of the strings within each model of instrument, and calculated such details as string tension and hammer strike position. He was also a highly-skilled tuner, voicer and regulator, as well as a fine classical pianist. His personality and his musical taste must have stamped themselves upon his firm's new instruments.[66]

Charles Squire was a member of another well-known London piano-making family. Shortly after the First War, Squire went into partnership with Clarence Lyon, and brought with him the brand name *Squire and Longson*. It would appear that the majority of instruments made at Medlar Street during the 1920s actually bore this trademark, although other names such as *Paul Newman, Ronson,* and of course *Welmar* would regularly appear on the pianos' nameboards, depending on the requirements of any particular dealer. All the pianos manufactured by Cremona Ltd may be identified by a large capital 'C' cast into their iron frames, followed by a model number. During the 1920s, the firm's range of uprights went from C20 (*circa* 1925) up to C30 (*circa* 1928), suggesting that the company was regularly introducing new designs during this period.[67]

Clarence Lyon with his wife Grace in the garden of their Dulwich home, London, mid 1920s.
[Photo: Donald Lyon]

Edmund de Gruchy Whomes (1878-1960), the third individual to be involved in the evolution of the Cremona/Welmar, was a piano dealer at Bexleyheath, Kent, and probably a stockist of Cremona instruments. The Whomes company had been established since 1865. Edmund Whomes had a particular interest in the design and construction of piano soundboards. Between 1927 and 1932, he experimented in the Cremona 'belly' shop with a new method of soundboard construction: in addition to shrinking the soundboards in a 'hot box' for a few days, prior to the ribs being attached, Whomes invented a clever device which actually subjected each soundboard to a sideways *crushing* force, so compressing the actual fibres of the timber from which the board was made. Whilst still locked in this sideways crushing 'grip', each board had its cluster of ribs quickly attached, using hot glue in a go-bar press.[68] The idea behind this unique process was to force the fibres of the soundboard to be in a *permanent* state of compression, locked in by the grip of the ribs, so that the board could never shrink – and therefore never split. This peculiar combination of shrinking and crushing gave the Cremona instruments an attractive 'intensity' of tone colour – which delighted the listener, and of course helped sales. Not surprisingly, Whomes' process was continued when all the various Cremona models became Welmar instruments from 1934, although the special process had been discontinued in the Clapham Park Road works by the late 1980s.

Alfred Knight (1899-1974), the fourth individual of the Cremona design team, later became very successful and highly regarded in his own right. His surname indeed became famous: it was to be seen on every Knight piano which left his own factory from July 1936. As a young man in his late twenties, Knight became under-manager at the Medlar Street works, and began to work with Clarence Lyon on the design and modification of new models. Knight's influence on the character of the firm's instruments may be seen from the late 1920s, when the latest upright models began to feature angular, girder-like iron frame designs, often with a highly-idiosyncratic long straight iron bar running the full width of the casting (a feature later to be seen in all of Knight's own upright instruments). The Medlar Street factory, with its enthusiasm for continuous experimentation, was certainly a perfect training ground for the young Alfred Knight. The experience he gained there

Opposite: Two 'Cremona' cast-iron frames, both from 1927, for the 'Squire and Longson' upright models. The upper photo shows the elegant and assured design of the C27. The lower photo shows a highly-unusual frame design (probably the handiwork of Alfred Knight) indicating an experimental move towards a 'girder type' construction in the Medlar Street works at this date.

[Photos: Booth and Brookes foundry archive, Essex Record Office, Chelmsford]

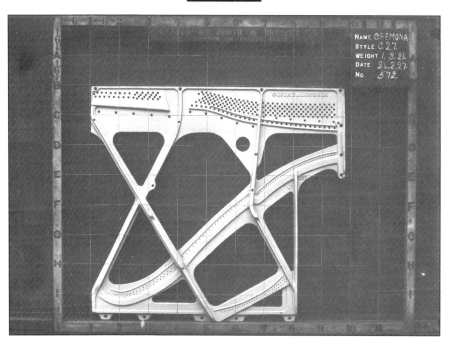

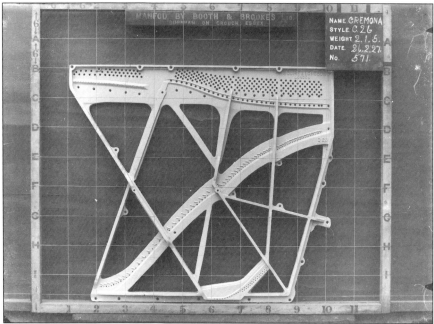

was doubtless of enormous value to him when he established his own factory a few years later.

The experimentation at Medlar Street also included new methods of applying the polish to the casework of the firm's pianos. The traditional hand polish – the so-called 'French polish' – was very labour-intensive to apply, and required a considerable amount of skill and time in order to build up a high-quality gloss surface, known in the furniture trade as a 'piano finish'. The application of lacquer by compressed air sprayer was a new, alternative method, borrowed from the car industry. For the directors of Cremona, its particular attraction lay in the way in which spraying achieved a high gloss finish in a much shorter time than the hand method, and so enabled the firm to reduce its manufacturing costs significantly.

Cremona Ltd is believed to have been the first in the piano industry to have attempted a spray finish. Very soon, all the other piano manufacturers followed. Many hand polishers were put out of work, and a generation of them became embittered because their skills had been jettisoned by their employers in such a hard-headed and hard-hearted manner. Those skilled polishers who remained with the piano industry were relegated to become humble groundwork 'colourers' or 'fillers in' of case parts, before those same parts were handed on to the spray polishers for finishing.

Instead of using the traditional alcohol-based shellac lacquer, Cremona began trials using sprayed cellulose. By all accounts, fire precautions with cellulose were quite slap-happy in the early days of its use; the dangers of such a volatile liquid were simply not appreciated, and the hazards of fires were significantly increased by the fact that most of the workforce in the 1920s would have been regular smokers. One morning in the year 1929, the Cremona employees arrived for work as usual – to find no factory there. The premises had been gutted in a ferocious fire, made worse by the explosive ignition of drums of cellulose lacquer. Piano manufacture in Medlar Street stopped abruptly, and the firm had to find temporary premises in order to continue with some kind of production. By the spring of 1931, however, the factory had been entirely rebuilt on its original site, and piano making resumed there.

Nevertheless, the Cremona company appears never to have recovered financially from the disruption, and after struggling on for a couple of years (it was still advertising its baby grand in July 1933) finally closed down in 1934.[69]

The closure of Cremona Ltd was obviously felt by Whelpdales, whose supply of new Welmar instruments came to a sudden halt. The loss was also seen as a tragedy within the industry, because the firm had made some extremely good pianos – and at a very reasonable and attractive price. The directors of Whelpdales therefore took steps to ensure the survival of all necessary designs, jigs, patterns and templates for the various Cremona models, moving these to a new manufacturing site a couple of miles to the south west, at 154 Clapham Park Road. Many of the former Cremona employees, along with Clarence Lyon himself, moved into the new premises. Lyon, whose long experience and expertise seemed to be an essential requirement in order to re-start production, was put in charge of the new factory, where employees were now instructed to continue with the production of Cremona-designed pianos – but bearing only one trademark: Welmar.

It must have been quite hard for Lyon to adjust to the new surroundings of Clapham Park Road, particularly as he was no longer the 'governor' of the business, but only a senior employee, receiving regular instructions from the firm's West End office. One day, so the legend has it, the directors, along with an important customer, decided to make an impromptu visit to the factory, a place they were not accustomed to visit very often. There, they found Lyon and his team hard at work making items of solid oak furniture for a local Baptist chapel where the Lyon family were leading members. This activity was not exactly in line with the company's declared policy of making pianos rather than pews. Lyon was hauled up to the West End offices and promptly dismissed. This must have happened at some point in the late 1940s. The Lyon family's continuity at Clapham Park Road was maintained, however, by Donald Lyon, Clarence's son, who for many years afterwards continued as the factory's storekeeper.

With the outbreak of the Second World War, manufacturing activities at the Clapham factory were greatly curtailed. The premises, however, was one of the two piano factories which was allowed to continue throughout the war years (the other was Alfred Knight's). Under the terms of the government's Concentration of Industry Act, three (rival) firms, John Broadwood and Sons Ltd, Sir Herbert Marshall and Sons Ltd and George Rogers and Sons Ltd moved into the Clapham factory and together were allowed to make a limited number of instruments under the same roof, alongside the customary Welmar production. It must have been a very curious time, during which an elderly workforce, perhaps suspicious of each other's skills, and exempt from active military service, endeavoured to maintain a trickle of piano production throughout the London Blitz. As an indication of the level of productivity during the War years, we can note that by 1947, shortly before the Broadwood company vacated the Clapham premises, the factory had completed seventy-two Broadwood upright instruments and one Broadwood baby grand, with a further eleven grands and thirty-eight uprights in the course of construction for the Broadwood firm.[70] These figures represented an output spread over a seven-year span.

In 1945, Sir Herbert Marshall and Sons Ltd, manufacturers of the *Marshall and Rose* piano, whose instruments had been made in the Clapham works throughout the War years, decided not to re-start their own production. Instead, the directors decided to sell their business to Whelpdales; and so from 1945, Marshall and Rose upright and grand pianos continued to be produced at Clapham, and soon formed approximately 20% of Whelpdale's annual output. The new Marshall and Rose models were internally identical to the Welmars; only small stylistic details to the external casework design distinguished one brand from the other.

The take-over of the long-established firm of Sir Herbert Marshall and Sons benefited Whelpdales in several ways. The company had been founded by a Leicester piano dealer, Joseph Herbert Marshall (1851-1918) who took over his father's bookshop in Rutland Street, Leicester, in 1882 and turned the premises into a highly successful piano showroom. Marshall's extrovert, charming and persuasive personality made him an excellent piano salesman. He moved into politics, becoming Lord Mayor of Leicester in 1896 (his knighthood was awarded for political services rather than for piano services). Marshall's huge ambition extended to piano manufacturing, and whilst remaining a resident of Leicester, he went into partnership in the year 1908 with George Rose, one of the most outstanding piano designers of his day, who had been a former director and factory manager of John Broadwood and Sons.[71]

Marshall and Rose pianos, expensive and high-quality items, were made in small numbers at the firm's factory in Prince of Wales' Road, Kentish Town, London. Although the original partnership lasted for only three years (Rose emigrated to Australia in 1911), the firm had begun to manufacture three large upright models and three sizes of grand, all to Rose's designs. By the early 1930s, the three original upright models had been discontinued, because they were far too tall and heavy for the furniture fashion of the period. At least one original Marshall and Rose model, however, the six-foot boudoir grand, remained in production throughout the 1930s (having had the

A six-foot Welmar grand in a special 'art deco' case of ash and walnut, despatched from Clapham Park Road on the 27th August 1948 for installation in the cruise ship Magdalena.
[Photo: David Locke collection]

style of its cast-iron frame modernised to the design of Alfred Knight). During the Second War, the wherewithal to make this particular model was of course moved into the Clapham works – and then appropriated by Whelpdales after 1945 when they themselves began to manufacture Marshall and Rose instruments. Before long, the same model was offered as a 'Welmar', and became a much-admired addition to the firm's fleet. It is certainly one of the finest medium-sized grands ever made in this country, comparable in tonal quality with two other good medium-length instruments of British manufacture: the Challen 19, and the similarly sized Chappell 'Mignon' model.

As well as enabling Whelpdales to expand their product range, the arrival of Marshall and Rose helped the company to widen its dealer network: there were many loyal Marshall dealers, particularly in the Leicester area and other parts of the Midlands, who would have been pleased to see the traditional Marshall and Rose quality being maintained at Clapham. There is a further benefit to consider: the fact that the company now had *two* trademarks available to the retail trade meant that it could supply its instruments to two different piano shops within the same town or city without infringing agency agreements. In Leeds between the 1950s and '70s, for example, the city's main piano shop, Barkers of the Headrow, was a Welmar stockist; in the suburbs, Douglas Hall of Chapeltown Road was a loyal Marshall and Rose retailer.

An overview of the Welmar baby grand piano, early 1950s. The piano's scale and frame design appear to be that of the Cremona model '4', in production from the early 1930s.

[Illustration from a Welmar publicity brochure]

Two other sizes of grand were available with either trademark after 1945: there was a small baby grand of length four foot nine inches, based on an earlier Cremona design dating from the early 1930s; and then a full-sized concert grand of nine foot length, of which only a few examples were produced, and therefore little impact was made on the British concert scene as a result – although one example was for many years the 'house piano' at Central Hall, Westminster. This concert instrument was apparently designed for

*The chunky casework features of a Welmar model 'C' upright, veneered in an
interesting decorative figured mahogany. Early 1950s.*
[Photo: Author's collection]

Whelpdales by Clarence Lyon during the mid to late 1940s. It would be
interesting to discover whether this new instrument was in fact based on the
design of an earlier Marshall and Rose model, utilising drawings, patterns and
jigs which are likely to have survived the War years. Of the three sizes of
Welmar or Marshall and Rose grand, only the six-foot boudoir model
remained in regular production by the late 1980s.[72]

Three main sizes of upright instrument were produced at Clapham from
1945: the models A, B and C. Internally, all of them were Cremona designs
dating back to the late 1920s or early '30s. (For example, the Cremona 'C 27'
strung back became the basis for the Welmar model 'B'). The little 'A' was
the firm's mainstay for many years, being produced in greater numbers than
any other model. In spite of its quite modest height (3' 7"), the 'A' has
noticeably long tenor string speaking lengths on a suspended bridge, helping
tonal clarity, and enabling the tuner to set a good temperament in the 'scale'

The small Welmar model 'A' upright, in the rather severe but elegant case style fashionable in the 1960s.

[Illustration from a Welmar publicity brochure]

area of the keyboard with ease. The bass section of this model is very satisfactory as well, considering the size of the instrument, provided that the wrapped copper on the wound bass strings is soft enough and has not been excessively work hardened, either during wire drawing or as a result of too-speedy core covering.

The largest Welmar upright of all, the imposing model B (later known as the 125 or 126 because its actual height is 125cm or 126cm) is an excellent instrument, but does not appear to have been made at all during the 1960s or even the '70s; however, the instrument was welcomed back into regular production from the 1980s, following an increase in demand for larger models which could compete with the new, significantly larger Yamaha uprights which were becoming increasingly seen in piano shops. Curious features of the 'B' are abnormally long backlengths of unstruck strings in the tenor and bass sections of the instrument. This must be a deliberate design feature.

It certainly results in a freer, responsive, resonant and more 'fluid' tonal character in this area of the model's compass.[73]

All three Welmar upright models have heavy, well-designed cast-iron frames and wooden braced backs. In fact, by the 1960s, the Whelpdale company was one of the few London makers who stubbornly continued to use substantial wooden back bracings at a time when fashion was moving towards cheaper, slimmer 'backless' instruments.[74] Whelpdales knew full well the acoustic and structural virtues of a properly-braced wooden back foundation for their uprights. However, at one period during the 1970s, the firm did break its usual rules, and manufactured one 'backless' upright: the model '41', a small budget piano of only 104cm height.

Throughout the 1950s and into the 1960s, the firm's works manager at Clapham, and Clarence Lyon's successor, was Sid Fosh, who as a tiny baby was given the remarkable name of Sidney Bechstein Fosh by his proud and piano-minded parents. It is not known how useful this second Christian name was for Mr Fosh's eventual career in the industry. Following his retirement, Fosh was succeeded by George McCrone, a New Zealander who had been working for the firm since 1946.

It was during McCrone's time that a significant change was made to the method of 'marking off' and preparing the soundboard bridges for the uprights: instead of being hand drilled, carved and then pinned *after* their attachment to their respective soundboards (which is the usual method), loose bridge cappings had their notches machined out on a table by a specially-jigged cutter – *before* being attached to their respective soundboards. Immediately after the cutting, all the steel bridge pins were rapidly fired in by a compressed air machine. Only after the bridge cappings had been carved and pinned in this way, were they then glued and screwed into place on lower bridge sections which had already been fixed to the soundboards. The independent bass bridges were constructed 'units' which were similarly carved and pinned before being glued and screwed into place.

The adjustment of the amount of string downbearing pressure on the bridges was achieved, not by planing off the tops of the bridges in the usual manner found in all other piano factories (this would of course have been impossible with the steel bridge pins already in place) but by controlling the downbearing angle of string backlength with cloth-covered bearing pads under the stringing. This method, unique to Welmar, was introduced in response to a worrying shortage of skills in the back-making department and as a time-saving device. In the words of McCrone: 'Used efficiently, the machinery for the drilling, carving and pinning of cappings and bass bridges produced a positive saving in marking-off time.' There was also no impairment to the tonal qualities of the various models as a result of the system's adoption.[75]

All the newly-designed marking-off machinery was housed in a room inside a single-storey, detached outbuilding in the main factory yard. This same building also housed the wood-converting machine shop and the casework veneering room. The advantage of isolating all these 'dusty' and swarf-producing processes in a self-contained outbuilding, so helping to keep the remainder of the factory relatively dust-free, can be readily appreciated. Bellying (soundboard making), backmaking and stringing was carried out on the ground floor of the main factory wing nearby, as was the bending of the grand rims; whilst upstairs at first-floor level in the same building the casework was fitted up, the actions and keys installed, and the instruments finally tuned and voiced before despatch.

The action regulator concentrates: Doug Sulley, Clapham Park Road, late 1980s.
[Photo: David Locke collection]

George McCrone retired in 1982, to be eventually succeeded in his role of technical supervisor by the 'two Davids' – David Oliver and David Locke. The former, who had completed a long technical apprenticeship with Steinways, was largely involved in the final checking over and passing out of the completed instruments before they left the factory. David Locke, having spent a number of years acquiring a high level of versatility by moving from department to department within the factory, was usually involved in the supervision of construction. In the course of his work he also carried out much-needed modifications and improvements to designs, jigs and templates.

A significant change to the settled atmosphere at Clapham Park Road took place in 1993, when, following the liquidation of the Bentley Piano Company Ltd of Woodchester Mills near Stroud, Gloucestershire, Whelpdales acquired by purchase the goodwill, trademarks, designs and manufacturing equipment of a range of upright pianos which bore a multitude of names: Bentley, Grover and Grover, Knight, Rogers, Steinberg, Hopkinson and Zender. The production of all these models moved from Woodchester up to Clapham, and Welmar's skilled factory staff were now faced with something of a headache: in addition to the three Welmar upright backs in regular production there, the London piano makers now had to adapt in order to work on a further *five* different designs of strung back, these being three Knights (K10, K46 and BK, used exclusively to make the Knight models) and two Bentley designs (SP41 and SP42), the latter two being used to make pianos bearing all the other brand names from Woodchester.

The chief complications arose from the fact that each of the three main marques – Welmar, Bentley and Knight – had their strung backs put together in rather different ways. The two Bentley backs, for example, were based on all-over iron frames without wooden back bracings, and their soundboard ribs were pre-shaped in order to achieve the desired curvature of the soundboard. Bentley string downbearing pressures were noticeably less than those found in the Knight and Welmar models. The Knights, like the Bentleys, had massive all-over cast frames, but retained wooden back bracings of sorts, mainly to protect their soundboards.

The Knight soundboard ribs, like those found in the Welmars, were *flat* rather than curved, but a specially-made press with a hollowed-out bed was used to glue the Knight ribs into place and achieve the necessary soundboard curvature at the same time. In contrast, the flat Welmar ribs were glued on to shrunken soundboards by way of 'go' bars' on a *flat* table. As we have already noted, the bridge notching and pinning on the Welmar uprights was carried out by a mechanical process unique to Welmar, whereas both the

Knight and Bentley models had their bridges marked off and pinned by hand only after these bridges were finally attached to their respective soundboards. At the beginning of these complicated times at Clapham Park Road, valuable practical help on the Knight instruments was received from Alfred Knight's grandson, Michael York, who had been familiar with their construction as a result of working in the family factory at Loughton, Essex.

It was not only in the backmaking department that complications arose: action finishers now had to take steps to tool-up for eight differing action and keyboard specifications instead of the former three. Eight slightly different types of keyboard now had to be ordered from the suppliers, with obvious reductions in economies of scale as a result. In retrospect, it might have made sense to have eliminated this kind of inefficiency, simply by reducing the range of strung backs manufactured to a bare minimum, and by choosing the most tonally satisfactory of the bunch for regular use.[76]

It was clearly the wish of the Welmar directors in 1993, however, to preserve some kind of real choice for the piano retailer. In particular, the Knight was a very individual kind of instrument, with a bright tone, very distinct from the Welmar's more mellow tonal qualities. Long-established and loyal Knight dealers would have wished for the continuity of this feature. The Bentleys, in spite of being for many decades among the cheapest pianos in the British trade, also had their own recognisable tonal characteristics, and were attractive to dealers because of their compact design and affordability. In persevering with the motley collection of designs at Clapham, Whelpdales were clearly endeavouring to offer to the retail Trade a spectrum of genuinely different kinds of instrument, so avoiding to some extent the much despised 'badge engineering'.

In spite of the obvious initial headaches caused by the incorporation of these extra designs into the routine production sequence, there were two decided advantages following on from all the changes: first of all, the employees' level of job interest would have been heightened, simply as a result of the much greater *variety* of pianos on the shop floor. And secondly, the unprecedented widening of the Whelpdale product range at this date would have maintained levels of output at Clapham, and would have helped to keep the workforce in full employment at a time when the London piano-manufacturing industry was clearly shrinking.

The continuity of manufacture at Clapham Park Road came under very serious threat in 2001: the landlords of the Welmar factory became

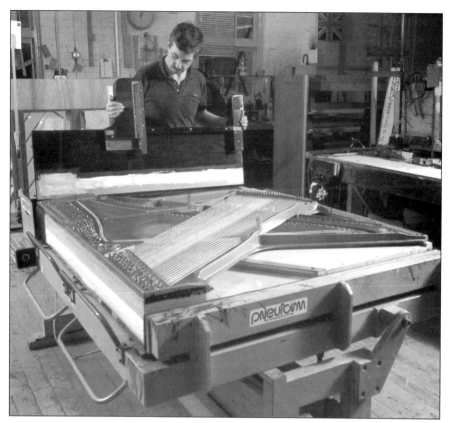

Bernard Weldon begins to glue on a treble case end to a strung back, Clapham Park Road.
[Photo: Cottage and Country *magazine, autumn 1990]*

increasingly aware of the high value of their occupied premises, not for use in manufacturing, but for development as housing accommodation in the form of flats, and the very large profits which could be reaped as a result. They proposed to Whelpdales a huge increase in rent – a proposal done as a 'lever' to try and force out their tenant. It was clearly the wish of the landlords that the piano makers should quit the premises. Rather than attempt to find alternative (and perhaps more compact) factory premises in south London, Whelpdales took the momentous decision to merge their resources with those of the Woodchester Piano Company, many miles away near Stroud in the west country. (Woodchester had taken over the former works premises of piano manufacturers Bentley, where many of the former Bentley employees still worked.)[77]

Discussions were entered into, and indeed at least six of the key personnel from London initially expressed interest in joining the team of Stroud piano makers. It was the intention that all essential jigs, templates, patterns and manufacturing equipment for the instruments, then in production at Clapham, should be moved down to the west country, and that a combined workforce there should continue the manufacture of Welmar, Knight and Bentley ranges in the former Bentley factory. As negotiations progressed, however, only one skilled Whelpdale employee, Bernard Weldon, a case fitter, ultimately decided to move down to the west country.

Now began a sad episode in the history of the Welmar piano, which lasted barely two years. If we are to analyse some of the causes of the failure of the Woodchester factory in the spring of 2003, at least two of them are clearly identifiable. First of all, there was tragically not enough transfer of highly-specialised and essential piano-making knowledge from London to Stroud. There was an unfortunate waste of time and materials as the Woodchester workforce struggled to understand the unfamiliar assembly of the various Welmar models. Secondly, for many decades the Clapham workforce had been making the most expensive British pianos; in contrast, the Woodchester factory had long prided itself on making much cheaper and more affordable instruments. The two 'schools' of piano making were not exactly compatible. Some of the fussy but critical procedures carried out at Clapham, such as the shrinking of soundboards in a 'hot box' prior to their ribs being attached, were simply not continued at Woodchester. In general, there was an acute shortage of skill, made worse as experienced senior members of staff began to be laid off in a cost-cutting exercise during the closing days of the company.

The end of the making of Welmar, Marshall & Rose, Knight and Bentley pianos in Britain was marked by the Official Receiver's public auction at the Woodchester factory on Wednesday 4th June 2003, when the stock of finished pianos was sold off. At the same auction, the author of this book was able to arrange the purchase of a considerable number of components for the Welmar 'A' and 'B' uprights. These items were exported to his own workshop, then in Norway, and over the next five years turned into completed instruments – but not, of course, bearing the *Welmar* name. A few weeks before the auction, the author had also acquired the rim-bending press necessary to manufacture the Welmar six-foot grand. This item was removed to Norway, arriving there in May 2003, where it remains in store in a piano workshop at Spikkestad, near Oslo.[78]

The well-known brand names associated with the Woodchester factory were purchased by a firm of importers, *Intermusic Ltd,* of Poole, Dorset. Very soon, Intermusic made arrangements to have the various trademarks affixed to instruments of Chinese manufacture. These imported pianos, of course, bear no resemblance to the original products formerly made at Clapham.

It is very much hoped that the long-established, well-tried Cremona/Welmar piano designs will, in the not-too-distant future, begin to form the basis of the production of new British-made pianos at the Broadwood workshops at Finchcocks, near Goudhurst in Kent. With luck, a new, younger generation of piano makers here will help to ensure the survival of piano-making skills in Britain throughout the twenty-first century.

*The Welmar six-foot grand rim press arrives at Moss, Norway,
early on a fine spring morning, May 2003.*
[Photo: Moss Avis]

NOTES

1. JOHN BRINSMEAD & SONS

1. Alfred Squire: article in *The British and Colonial Piano Journal,* December 1904.

2. A printed Bechstein publicity brochure of *circa* 1900 has forty-three royal heads of state name-dropped on its title page as being the firm's customers. *(Author's collection.)*

3. Source: see note 1 (above).

4. The highly-valuable publication, *Pierce Piano Atlas,* contains lists of production serial numbers and dates for all leading European and American piano manufacturers. From the *Atlas,* it is often possible to estimate the level of output of any firm (viz: numbers of pianos made each year), as well as being able to establish the approximate age of any particular instrument. Unfortunately, the *Atlas* has many careless printing errors, and so the information it contains must be treated with caution. Published by Larry E. Ashley, Albuquerque, New Mexico 87154-0520, USA.

5. Company archive of John Broadwood and Sons Ltd, now housed at Surrey History Centre, Woking, Surrey. The reference to the Brinsmead sale is found in ledger 2185/JB/29/46/1-2.

6. See an extract from a letter written by the concert pianist Clara Schumann, which is quoted in Dieter Hilderbrandt's *Piano Forte: A Social History,* page 144. Published by Hutchinson, London, 1985. (However, the date of the letter is not given.)

7. Rosa Brinsmead (Mrs Billinghurst) was in fact a highly-gifted pianist and composer. One of her charming keyboard compositions, *Barcarolle*, was published by Augener and Company. *(Source of information: Patrick and Ann Billinghurst.)*

8. The firm of J. & J. Goddard, known as 'The Home of Piano Supplies' was founded in the year 1842 by Joseph Goddard (died 1889) who entered into partnership with his brother James in the year 1849. The firm began as ironmongers to the piano trade, later branching out into wound bass string manufacture and the supply of felt and cloth. We assume that 'Tom' Brinsmead had married a daughter of Joseph Goddard. The firm not only had ties with members of the Brinsmead family: during the 1950s and '60s, Harry Marcy Collard, formerly of Collard and Collard, was active as a director. From around the year 1970, the firm of Goddards was taken over by Wallgate and Company, and the Tottenham Court Road shop was closed. Wallgate in turn became part of the Naish Group of felt distributors, today based at Wilton, Wiltshire.

9. British Patent, 12th May 1885, taken out in the name of 'John Brinsmead'.

10. A Brinsmead brochure of *circa* 1900 lists:

> Concert grand, 8 feet long.
> Small concert grand (7' 3")
> Boudoir grand (6' 3")
> Baby grand (5')
> Overstrung uprights (4' 6", 4' 3", 4' 2" and 3' 11" height)
> Oblique-strung upright (3' 11")
> Straight-strung uprights (4' 6" and 4' 3" height)
>
> *(Information from George Brinsmead, California, USA.)*

11. Information obtained from documents provided by Chris and Coral Brinsmead, and Sue Christian.

12. Printed minutes of the Annual General Meeting of John Brinsmead and Sons Ltd, 31st December 1917 *(Source: Patrick and Ann Billinghurst.)*

13. Source as note 12 (above).

14. Details from various articles which appeared in *The Pianomaker,* a monthly trade journal, during the year 1921. Editor: Herbert Sinclair.

15. Patrick and Ann Billinghurst in conversation with the author, 2008.

16. The apprenticeship indenture of William Sale of 22 Brownlow Road, Dalston, London. *(Author's collection.)*

17. Cyril Ehrlich: *The Piano. A History,* pages 148-149. Published by J. M. Dent and Sons Ltd, London, 1976.

18. William Sale, in conversation with the author, *circa* 1970.

2. CHALLEN

19. Details about Watlen and Challen supplied by Bill Kibby, *The Piano History Centre,* 271, Southtown Road, Great Yarmouth NR31 0JB.

20. Peter Challen, in conversation with the author, *circa* 1986.

21. Alfred Dolge: *Pianos and Their Makers,* page 247. Covina Publishing Company, Covina, California, USA, 1911.

22. Miss Katherine M. Challen, in conversation with the author, 1983.

Sydney A. Hurren, OBE.
[Photo from The Pianomaker, *circa 1920]*

23. Sydney Alfred Hurren, OBE (1886-1964), a native of Yoxford, Suffolk, and a fine pianist, trained as a schoolteacher at Saltley College, Birmingham. According to Hurren's daughter, Dr C. E. Presswood, her father 'had a dream-vision that he would one day work for the British piano trade and overcome the contemporary preference for German instruments'. After the First World War, Hurren was appointed lecturer at the Music Trades School, based at the Northern Polytechnic, Holloway Road, where his speciality was the teaching of piano scale design. The improvement to the interior design of London-made pianos as a result of his tireless work 'behind the scenes' is hard to estimate because of a lack of evidence, but a number of leading manufacturers (Challen and Danemann for example) owed a great debt to his teaching skills. Sydney Hurren was awarded the OBE in 1949 for services to the piano industry.

Samuel Wolfenden (1846-1929) was also a lecturer in piano technology at the Northern Polytechnic, probably on a part-time basis, as he had retired by 1916. He had had many years' practical experience in the industry as a maker and designer, working initially for the firm of George Rogers and Sons, and then for the American-owned Orchestrelle Company of Hayes, makers of the *Steck* and *Aeolian* pianos. Wolfenden's valuable publication *A Treatise on the Art of Pianoforte Construction* was published by Unwin Brothers Ltd in 1916. This was followed by *A Supplement to A Treatise on Pianoforte Construction,* published by King and Jarrett in 1927. The latter publication contains fascinating practical information about soundboard making.

24. Mrs Margaret Wolfe-Barry, in conversation with the author, 2009.

25. The Purchase Records of Wigmore Hall Galleries, Wigmore Street, London, 1916-1966. *(Author's collection.)*

26. Production statistics from *Pierce Piano Atlas* (see note 4).

27. Sydney Paradine, a former Chappell tuner in the Ferdinand Street factory, in conversation with the author, *circa* 1980.

28. From the pages of *The Pianomaker* journal, 1934 (see note 14).

Samuel Wolfenden, photographed in 1925 with his machine for testing the strength of piano wire.
[Photo from The Pianomaker]

29. For further details see: Alastair Laurence: *The Broadwood Barless Piano. A History.* Pioneer Press, Skipton, 2004.

30. *Pierce Piano Atlas.*

31. The last will and testament of Willie Evans of 'West Garth', 8 Western Avenue, Branksome Park, Poole, Dorset, made 17th September 1979, proved 6th October 1980. (York Probate Registry.)

32. The author of this book was working in the Challen/Brasted factory in 1969.

33. The rim-bending equipment for the Challen 16 model is on public display each Sunday afternoon from Easter until the end of September at Finchcocks Musical Museum, Goudhurst, Kent TN17 1HH.

3. COLLARD & COLLARD

34. Serial numbers in *Pierce Piano Atlas* (note 4).

35. F. W. Collard's obituary in the *Illustrated London News,* 11th February 1860.

36. See the highly-detailed and well-researched article by Jenny Nex: 'Culliford and Company', which appears in *Early Keyboard Journal,* volume 22, published in 2004 by the Southeastern Historical Keyboard Society, Columbia, South Carolina, USA.

37. Jenny Nex, an authority on the firm of Longman and Broderip, will contribute a chapter based on her researches to the forthcoming book, *The London Music Trade* (editor: Michael Kassler), to be published by Ashgate, summer 2010.

38. The Clementi letters, John Collard's family archive.

39. The two grands in question form part of Richard Burnett's Collection, housed at Finchcocks Musical Museum, Goudhurst, Kent, where they may be seen, played and compared.

40. See: David Wainwright: *Broadwood by Appointment,* page 108. Quiller Press, London, 1982.

41. A useful study of the Clementi serial numbering system was undertaken by Leif Sahlquist of Malmo, Sweden, in 2004. Sahlquist has pointed out the significance of the firm's serial numbers for grands and squares around the year 1807, and his analysis shows a disruption to square production, rather than grands, as a result of the factory fire.

42. British Patents, 3481.

43. The invention of the upright grand action is attributed to Robert Stodart, the Dalkeith engineer and grand piano maker who left Scotland and who had settled in London by the 1780s. According to a legend handed down through the Stodart family, Robert Stodart was sitting in church one Sunday morning, listening to a long and dull sermon, when he suddenly realised in a flash how an *upright* grand action mechanism could be constructed. On impulse, he jumped up in his pew and ran out of the church at high speed, much to the amazement of the congregation. On reaching home, Stodart immediately set to work, building a one-note working model for his design. (However, Stodart's upright grand action mechanism appears to have been patented by a certain *William* Stodart, Robert's nephew, in 1795; and this in turn was preceded by a very similar action patented by the London maker John Landreth in 1787. If Robert Stodart *did* contribute ideas towards these patented designs, then unfortunately we have no evidence to prove it.) See also: Rosamond E. M. Harding: *The Pianoforte,* pages 60-63. Cambridge University Press, 1933.

44. British Patents, 4542.

45. British Patents, 5475.

46. *Pierce Piano Atlas.*

47. A printed advertisement for this concert, listing the items to be performed, is part of the archive of the Royal College of Music, London.

48. *Goad's Fire Insurance Map,* 1891. (Camden Local Studies Library, Holborn.)

49. Information received from John Collard.

50. Horace Singleton, in conversation with the author, early 1970s.

51. Details from an obituary of Charles Lukey Collard, which appeared in *Musical Opinion and Music Trade Review,* January 1892.

52. Cecil Collard's 'celeste' pedal system for the grand is British Patents 3595, dated 18th August 1881. It would be interesting to hear a Collard grand incorporating this feature.

53. *Pierce Piano Atlas.*

54. The will of John Clementi Collard of 25 Hamilton Terrace, London N.W., dated the 14th November 1917 and proved on 20th November 1918. (York Probate Registry.)

55. The author's great-uncle, Herbert Laurence (1867-1922), was apprenticed in Kirkman's Hammersmith factory.

56. Information from the Swedish State Archives, Gothenburg, where the bankruptcy papers are preserved.

57. Information received from John Collard.

58. This story was told by Harry Collard to Charles Gilbey, who later re-told it to the author.

59. These two models are the only ones shown to be available in a Collard & Collard advertising leaflet dating from the 1960s. *(Author's collection.)*

4. W. DANEMANN & COMPANY

60. The story of the origins of the firm comes from Edgar Danemann, in conversation with the author, *circa* 1972.

61. A copy of the 1934 Agreement is in the author's collection.

62. The handwritten scale-design notebooks of Peter Danemann, now in the author's collection.

63. Tim Danemann Pianos, Unit 22, Dart Mills, Buckfastleigh, Devon TQ11 0NF.

64. Information about the Cardiff Danemanns received from Steve and Jeff Gardner, Gardner Pianos, 266 North Road, Cardiff CF14 3BL.

5. WELMAR

65. Rosamond Harding, *The Pianoforte,* page 399 (see note 43).

66. Information received from Donald Lyon, 1984.

67. Details obtained from the company archives of Booth and Brookes, ironfounders, who were the manufacturers of Cremona's cast-iron piano frames during the 1920s and '30s. The foundry was at Burnham-on-Crouch, Essex, and closed down around the year 1980. This firm's extensive archives were then deposited by Patrick Booth into the safe keeping of the Essex County Record Office, Chelmsford. Of particular interest in the archive is a large collection of photographs of piano frames.

68. Information received from Edmund Whomes junior, 1985.

69. The Cremona baby grand was advertised in the July 1933 issue of *The Pianomaker.*

70. John Broadwood and Sons Ltd Company archive, Finchcocks, Goudhurst, Kent.

71. Alastair Laurence: *The Broadwood Barless Piano. A History,* pages 17-25 (see note 29).

72. A recommended retail price dated January 1987 shows the Welmar six-foot model as the only grand offered at that date, finished in a black polyester case and costing £9,672 including VAT. This compares with the figure of £12,690 for the same-sized imported Blüthner in an identical finish.

73. The 'backlengths' are the distances between the bridge pins on the mainbridge and the hitchpins on the iron frame, where the strings terminate. A longer string backlength reduces the 'clamping' effect on the soundboard as the strings pass over the soundboard bridge. A typical 'standard' backlength is between 5 and 8cm. The Welmar 'B' upright design has backlengths in its tenor and bass of up to 25cm.

74. British piano manufacturers who had gone 'backless' by the 1960s included: Ajello, Barratt and Robinson, Bentley, Brasted, Challen, Kemble, Renn, Rogers, and Zender. The backless idea was essentially a way of reducing manufacturing costs, and was adopted by makers of smaller, 'budget' uprights. The traditional and more expensive wooden braced back was retained by Broadwood, Danemann and Knight, as well as Welmar. At the same period, Monington & Weston made good-toned (but very heavy) pianos with *cast iron* back bracings. In theory, a well-constructed wooden braced back gives a more stable foundation for the casework, enhances the tonal quality of the instrument, and enables more string downbearing pressure to be safely brought to the soundboard. 'Backless' instruments are usually obliged to be made with less string downbearing pressure. Yamaha and Kawai uprights, imported into Britain from Japan from the 1960s, all have substantial wooden back bracings.

75. Information received from George McCrone, 2009.

76. Exactly this process happened in the Chappell piano factory in Camden Town during the 1930s, when an assortment of well-established Collard, Kirkman, Allison and Strohmenger upright back designs, which had been acquired by the Chappell Piano Company Ltd, were all scrapped in favour of two or three sizes of new Chappell backs, designed by Ernest Gowland, around which all the various brands were thereafter constructed. Information from Sydney Paradine (see note 27).

77. The details in this paragraph were received from Roger Willson.

78. At the time of the printing of this book, it is planned to move this well-travelled rim-bending apparatus back to England.

APPENDIX 1
Checklist of John Brinsmead & Sons Awards, 1862–1897

1862 London: Inventions Exhibition: bronze medal.

1869 Amsterdam, Holland: Internationale Exhibition: bronze medal.

1870 Paris: Académie Nationale Agricole Manufacturière et Commerciale: gold medal.

1876 Philadelphia, USA: International Exhibition: bronze medal.

1877 Port Elizabeth: South Africa Exhibition: silver medal.

1878 Paris: Académie Nationale Agricole Manufacturière et Commerciale: gold medal.

1879 Sydney, Australia: International Exhibition: bronze medal.

1880 Melbourne, Australia: International Exhibition: gold medal.

1880 Queensland, Australia: National Agricultural and Industrial Association of Queensland: gold medal.

1883 Cork, Ireland: Industrial Exhibition: bronze medal.

1883-4 Calcutta, India: International Exhibition: gold medal.

1885 Antwerp, Belgium: Exposition Universelle: gold medal.

1885 London: International Inventions Exhibition: silver medal.

1888 Barcelona, Spain: Exposición Universal de Barcelona: bronze medal.

1891 Jamaica: International Exhibition: bronze medal.

1894 Queensland, Australia: The National Agricultural and Industrial Association of Queensland: silver medal.

1894-5 Hobart, Tasmania: International Exhibition: gold medal.

1897 Queensland, Australia: International Exhibition: gold medal.

(Information provided by Patrick and Ann Billinghurst)

APPENDIX 2
An outline tree of the CHALLEN family of piano makers

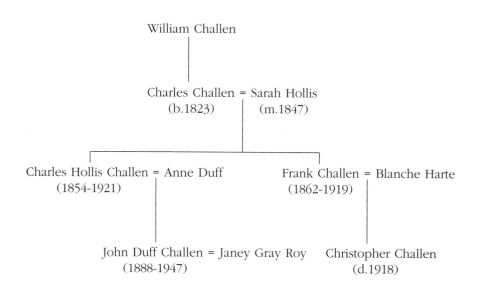

William Challen

Charles Challen = Sarah Hollis
(b.1823)   (m.1847)

Charles Hollis Challen = Anne Duff   Frank Challen = Blanche Harte
(1854-1921)   (1862-1919)

John Duff Challen = Janey Gray Roy   Christopher Challen
(1888-1947)   (d.1918)

APPENDIX 3
Challen's grand range, 1930–1936

LENGTH: 4' 0" (122cm) model 29: *'Diminutive'* or *'Challenette'*

4' 3" (129.5cm) model 21: *'Petite grand'*

4' 3" (129.5cm) model 26 double overstrung: *'Petite grand'*

4' 6" (137cm) model 23: *'Miniature grand'*

4' 6" (137cm) model 24 double overstrung: *'Miniature grand'*

5' 0" (152.5cm) model 16: *'Baby grand'*

6' 4" (193cm) model 19: *'Boudoir grand'*

8' 0" (244cm) model 18: *'Concert grand'*

10' 0" (305cm): *'Large concert grand'*

12' 0" (366cm): *'Largest grand in the World'*

(Apart from the model '16', which dates from the early 1920s, all the above models were newly-introduced in the period 1930-36)

APPENDIX 4
An outline tree of the COLLARD family of piano makers
Those members with their surnames shown in capitals were active in the piano industry

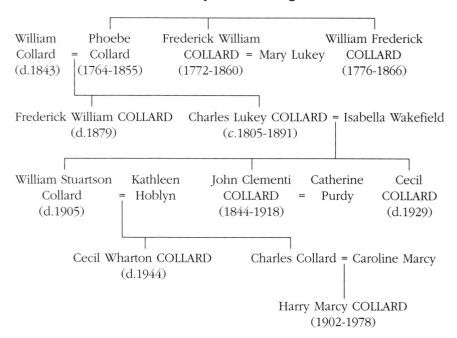

William
Collard
(d.1843)

Phoebe
= Collard
(1764-1855)

Frederick William
COLLARD = Mary Lukey
(1772-1860)

William Frederick
COLLARD
(1776-1866)

Frederick William COLLARD
(d.1879)

Charles Lukey COLLARD = Isabella Wakefield
(c.1805-1891)

William Stuartson
Collard
(d.1905)

Kathleen
= Hoblyn

John Clementi
COLLARD
(1844-1918)

Catherine
= Purdy

Cecil
COLLARD
(d.1929)

Cecil Wharton COLLARD
(d.1944)

Charles Collard = Caroline Marcy

Harry Marcy COLLARD
(1902-1978)

APPENDIX 5
The 'Pohlmann' upright scale as used by W. Danemann & Company from 1934

The first column gives the names of the notes, the second column gives their string speaking lengths in centimetres, the third shows the changes in wire gauges, and the fourth indicates the fraction of selected speaking lengths where the hammer strikes. *(Source: Peter Danemann's scale design notes.)*

c88	5.20cm	($13^1/_2$ gauge)	
b87	5.55	,,	
a#86	5.90	,,	
a85	6.25	,,	
g#84	6.60	,,	
g83	7.02	,, ...fourteenth	
f#82	7.40	,,	
f81	7.64	(14 gauge) ....thirteenth	
e80	8.05	,,	
d#79	8.60	,,	
d78	9.10	,, ...twelfth	
c#77	9.65	,,	
c76	10.15	,,	
b75	10.45	($14^1/_2$ gauge) ....eleventh	
a#74	11.08	,,	
a73	11.75	,,	

g#72	12.42	,,
g71	13.20	,,
f#70	13.97	,,
f69	14.40	(15 gauge).....................................tenth
e68	15.22	,,
d#67	16.15	,,
d66	17.11	,,
c#65	18.15	,,
c64	19.20	,,
b63	19.72	($15^1/_2$ gauge)
a#62	20.92	,,
a61	22.22	,,
g#60	23.52	,,
g59	24.95	,,
f#58	26.50	,,
f57	27.20	(16 gauge)
e56	28.90	,,..ninth
d#55	30.56	,,
d54	32.50	,,
c#53	34.35	,,
c52	36.40	,,
b51	37.50	($16^1/_2$ gauge)
a#50	39.80	,,
a49	42.20	,,
g#48	44.70	,,
g47	47.30	,,
f#46	50.10	,,...eighth
f45	51.80	(17 gauge)
e44	54.80	,,
d#43	58.20	,,
d42	61.60	,,
c#41	63.70	($17^1/_2$ gauge)
c40	67.30	,,
b39	69.70	,,
a#38	73.80	(18 gauge)....................................eighth
a37	76.30	($18^1/_2$ gauge)
g#36	79.00	(19 gauge)
g35	81.90	($19^1/_2$ gauge) ....eighth
f#34	84.90	(20 gauge)
f33	88.10	($20^1/_2$ gauge)
e32	89.50	(21 gauge)

d#31 and below: copper over-wound bass strings.

APPENDIX 6
The Welmar model 'B' upright piano soundboard

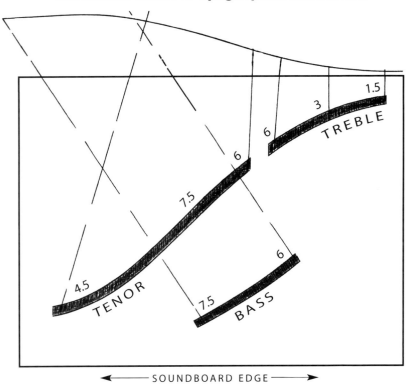

The diagram opposite shows the portions of total wooden bridge height (in millimetres) which are carefully calculated during manufacture to be *higher* than a straight string line drawn between the iron top bridge and the iron hitch plate. The greater bridge height in the central area is necessary to compensate for a greater degree of soundboard sinking or 'yield' in this vicinity as a result of string downbearing pressure.

(Measurements supplied by David Holmes.)

APPENDIX 7
Government Census Return for London, 1921:
Those employed in Musical Instrument Trades

	MALES	FEMALES
Makers of musical instruments:	6,690	637
Employers and managers:	237	4
Foremen and overlookers:	60	7
Action makers, fitters and assemblers:	370	143
Piano tuners:	758	3
Other workers:	305	142

INDEXES

TECHNICAL INDEX

FACTORIES INDEX

All addresses marked (L) are in London